A GIFT FOR

FROM

OUR DAILY Bread

COUNTRYMAN

Copyright © 2004 by Discovery House Publishers.

Published by the J. Countryman division of the Thomas Nelson Book Group,
Nashville, Tennessee 37214.

This book is based upon selections from *Our Daily Bread,*
Copyright ©1988 to 2001 by RBC Ministries, and is published by
special arrangement with and permission of Discovery House Publishers,
3000 Kraft Avenue, SE, Grand Rapids, Michigan, 49512. All rights reserved.

Compiled and edited by Terri Gibbs.
Project Manager: Michelle Orr

Unless otherwise indicated, all Scripture quotations in this book are from
The New King James Version (NKJV) ©1979, 1980, 1982, 1992,
Thomas Nelson, Inc., Publisher. Used by permission.

www.thomasnelson.com
www.jcountryman.com

Designed by LeftCoast Design, Portland, Oregon.

ISBN: 1-4041-0098-9

Printed and bound in Belgium

Writers

Henry G. Bosch
(1914–1995)

J. David Branon

David L. Burnham

Dennis J. De Haan

M. R. De Haan, M.D.
(1891–1965)

Martin R. De Haan II

Richard W. De Haan
(1923-2002)

David C. Egner

Vernon C. Grounds

David C. McCasland

Haddon W. Robinson

David H. Roper

Herbert Vander Lugt

Paul R. Van Gorder

Joanie E. Yoder

WHEN READING GOD'S WORD, TAKE SPECIAL CARE

TO FIND THE RICH TREASURES HIDDEN THERE;

GIVE THOUGHT TO EACH LINE, EACH PRECEPT HEAR,

THEN PRACTICE IT WELL WITH GODLY FEAR.

ANONYMOUS

January

Teach us to number our days,
that we may gain a heart of wisdom.

PSALM 90:12

A high school teacher in Los Angeles had a unique way of stimulating her students to think. From time to time she would write brief messages on the chalkboard that were unrelated to their current studies.

One morning, the students found the number 25,550 written on the board. One pupil finally raised his hand and asked the instructor why that particular number was there. She explained that 25,550 represented the number of days in the life of a person who lives to be 70. The teacher was trying to emphasize life's brevity and the value of each day.

It's important that we make the most of our opportunities to honor God, serve others, and proclaim Christ. Let's ask God to "teach us to number our days" so we will spend them wisely! —R. W. D.

DON'T JUST SPEND TIME; INVEST IT.

The purpose of the commandment is love from a pure heart,
from a good conscience, and from sincere faith.

1 TIMOTHY 1:5

When you set sail on the high seas, you need to know three important facts: your location, your destination, and your course. By referring to a map and using a compass, you can end up where you want to go.

The hard part comes in determining where you are at any given moment. Foul weather creates conditions that can sometimes confuse sailors. I heard about someone who set out across Lake Michigan from Milwaukee to Grand Haven. After sailing for 2 hours, trusting his own sense of direction, he spotted a large city on the horizon—Milwaukee! Somehow, thinking he was headed east, he had gone in a huge circle.

How does a follower of Christ stay on course and avoid spiritual shipwreck? By carefully reading and following the directions in God's Word, depending on the Spirit's leading, and listening to the wise counsel of Christian friends. —D. C. E.

TO STAY ON COURSE, TRUST THE COMPASS OF GOD'S WORD.

He who sows sparingly will also reap sparingly, and
he who sows bountifully will also reap bountifully.

2 CORINTHIANS 9:6

On my father's farm were certain fields he sowed by hand. He would strap on a canvas contraption that looked somewhat like a kangaroo pouch, fill it with seed, and go out to sow. He would cast seed everywhere.

When a farmer sows seed in his field, it looks like he's throwing it away. It seems to be lost, but it isn't really gone. In due time he gets it back—with much more besides.

When we give ourselves to Christ, it may seem to people as if we're throwing our life away. But Jesus teaches us to measure our lives by losses rather than gains, by sacrifices rather than self-preservation, by time spent for others rather than time lavished upon ourselves, by love poured out rather than love poured in. —D. H. R.

WHEN YOU GRASP, YOU LOSE; WHEN YOU GIVE TO GOD, YOU GAIN.

If you keep My commandments, you will abide in My love.

JOHN 15:10

In his book *The Best Is Yet To Be*, Henry Durbanville told the story of a little girl in London who won a prize at a flower show. Her entry was grown in an old cracked teapot and had been placed in the rear attic window of a rundown tenement house. When asked how she managed to raise such a lovely flower in such an unlikely environment, she said she moved it around so it would always be in the sunlight.

Durbanville then reminded his readers of Jesus' words, "As the Father loved Me, I also have loved you; abide in My love" (John 15:9). We, too, must keep ourselves continually in the warmth of Christ's love. We abide in His love when we show love to others. That's the way to stay in the sunshine! —R. W. D.

OUR LOVE FOR GOD IS SEEN IN OUR LOVE FOR OTHERS.

Who is the man that fears the LORD?
Him shall He teach in the way He chooses.

PSALM 25:12

At the University of Santa Clara, California, a researcher conducted a study of 1500 business managers to determine, among other things, what workers value most in a boss. The survey revealed that employees respect leaders who are competent, have the ability to inspire, and are skillful in providing direction. But there was a fourth quality they admired even more—integrity. Above all else, workers wanted managers who kept their word, who were honest, who were trustworthy.

While this finding holds special significance for Christian managers, it also says something to all who name the name of Christ. Integrity is a trait that applies to all believers, no matter what their position. It should be at the very heart of every word and deed of every godly person. Since the God of the Bible always keeps His word, it follows that godly people should also be known as those who do what they say they will do. —M. R. D. II

THOSE WHO ARE ON THE LEVEL CAN RISE TO THE HIGHEST PLACE.

Your word I have hidden in my heart,
that I might not sin against You.

PSALM 119:11

Michael Billester, a Bible distributor, visited a small hamlet in Poland shortly before World War II and gave a Bible to a villager who read it and was converted. The new believer then passed the Book on to others. The cycle of conversions and sharing continued until two hundred people had become believers through that one Bible. When Billester returned in 1940, this group of Christians met together for a worship service and asked him to preach the Word. He normally asked for testimonies, but this time he suggested that several in the audience recite verses of Scripture. One man stood and said, "Perhaps we have misunderstood. Did you mean verses or chapters?"

The villagers had not memorized a few selected verses of the Bible but whole chapters and books. Transformed lives bore witness to the power of the Word. To experience for ourselves the Bible's transforming power, we must read and memorize it and apply its truth daily. —P. R. V.

TOO MANY PEOPLE PUT THE BIBLE ON
THE SHELF INSTEAD OF IN THEIR HEARTS.

They could find no charge or fault,
because he was faithful.

DANIEL 6:4

A young man was being interviewed for a position in a small business firm. The applicant had a neat appearance and made a good impression on the owner. He had also prepared an excellent resumé in which he listed, as references, his pastor, his Sunday school teacher, and a church deacon. The owner of the business studied the resumé for several minutes, then said, "I appreciate these recommendations from your church friends. But what I would really like is word from someone who knows you on weekdays."

Sorry to say, in too many instances there is a striking contrast between the behavior of Christians in church and out in the world. The principles we hear preached on Sunday should be practiced all week. A good Sunday Christian will also be a good weekday Christian.
—R. W. D.

A HYPOCRITE IS A PERSON WHO IS NOT HIMSELF ON SUNDAY.

And the rain descended, . . . and the winds
blew and beat on that house; and it fell.

MATTHEW 7:27

A heavy rain had stopped falling just before a man drove down a lonely road. As he rounded a curve, he saw an old farmer surveying the ruins of his barn. The driver stopped to ask what happened. "Roof fell in," said the farmer. "Leaked so long it just rotted clear through." "Why didn't you fix it before it got so bad?" asked the stranger. "Well, sir," replied the farmer, "I just never seemed to get around to it. When the weather was good, I didn't need to. And when it rained, it was too wet to work on!"

It's easy to think, someday I'll take care of those little sinful habits; someday I'll start living for Christ. Such an attitude is no different from that of the farmer. Jesus said, "Therefore whoever hears these sayings of Mine, and does them, I will liken him to a wise man who built his house on the rock" (Matt. 7:24).

We grow strong in character by applying God's Word to our daily activities. —D. J. D.

THE CHARACTER WE BUILD IN THIS WORLD WE CARRY INTO THE NEXT.

*Our light affliction . . . is working for us
a far more exceeding . . . weight of glory.*

2 CORINTHIANS 4:17

In his book *Cheer Up*, August Van Ryn tells a story about a delivery truck that stopped at a house on a wintry day. Snow and ice covered the front steps. As the driver ran up the stairs to tell the resident he had a delivery, he slipped and fell. Picking himself up, he rang the doorbell, returned to the truck, and picked up the heavy trunk he was to deliver. With its weight on his shoulders, he was able to walk up the steps without slipping. The load on his back not only weighed him down; it also kept him up.

At times our load seems too heavy, but God is using it to keep us on a firm footing. He is building character and conforming us to the image of His Son. Our weight of trouble may seem oppressive, but it doesn't have to be. It can be God's method of keeping us dependent upon Him. —P. R. V.

GOD SENDS TRIALS NOT TO IMPAIR US BUT TO IMPROVE US.

When wisdom enters your heart, . . . discretion will preserve you.

PROVERBS 2:10–11

Toward the close of World War II, one Allied unit was assigned a crucial mission in Berlin. Each soldier had to memorize a map detailing all of Berlin's important military sites—in a single night! In just a few hours, each soldier had committed the map to memory. The mission was a success.

Several years later, the Army conducted an experiment to see if that original feat could be duplicated. They offered a similar unit an extra week's furlough—an attractive incentive—if they could carry out a comparable mission without a hitch. But the second unit could not match the success of the first. What made the difference? The lives of the men were not at stake.

Christians are engaged in spiritual warfare (Eph. 6:10–18). Our road map, our plan of strategy against Satan's military strongholds, is the Bible. The more of it we memorize, and the more thoroughly we know it, the more effective we will be for God. —H. W. R.

**IF YOUR LIFE DEPENDED ON KNOWING THE BIBLE,
HOW LONG WOULD YOU LAST?**

*Daniel . . . knelt down on his knees three times that day,
and prayed and gave thanks before his God.*

DANIEL 6:10

Have you ever wondered why a pigeon walks so funny? It's so that it can see where it's going. Because a pigeon's eyes can't focus as it moves, the bird actually has to bring its head to a complete stop between steps in order to refocus. So it proceeds clumsily—head forward, stop, head back, stop.

In our spiritual walk with the Lord, we have the same problem as the pigeon: We have a hard time seeing while we're on the go. We need to stop between steps—to refocus on the Word and the will of God. That's not to say we have to pray and meditate about every little decision in life. But certainly our walk with the Lord needs to have built into it a pattern of stops that enable us to see more clearly before moving on. —M. R. D. II

TIME IN CHRIST'S SERVICE REQUIRES TIME OUT FOR RENEWAL.

Rest in the LORD, and wait patiently for Him.

PSALM 37:7

The great preacher Phillips Brooks was noted for his poise and quiet manner. At times, however, he suffered moments of frustration and irritability. One day a friend saw him pacing the floor like a caged lion. "What's the trouble, Dr. Brooks?" asked the friend. "The trouble is that I am in a hurry," said Brooks, "but God isn't." Haven't we often felt the same?

Jonathan Goforth (1859–1936), a missionary to China, was convinced that the city of Changte should be his field of spiritual labor. But his faith was severely tested as he was mobbed and threatened when visiting the city. Finally, after 6 frustrating years, permission to begin his work was granted. Within 3 days of reaching Changte he had received no less than 35 offers of land, among them the very site he had chosen earlier as the most ideal spot for the mission. Wait patiently for the Lord. He will give you what's best— in His time! —H. G. B.

GOD IS NEVER IN A HURRY, BUT HE IS ALWAYS ON TIME.

You shall be witnesses to Me in Jerusalem, and in all
Judea and Samaria, and to the end of the earth.

ACTS 1:8

here are two kinds of people when it comes to missions
—those who need to share Christ and those who need to
hear about Christ.

H. A. Ironside used to tell about a meeting in which a missionary
offering was taken. When the collection plate was handed to a wealthy
man, he brushed it aside and said, "I do not believe in missions."
"Then take something out," said the usher. "This is for the heathen."

Every Christian is part of Christ's mission in the world. What
Jesus told His disciples in Acts 1 applies also to us. We are His
witnesses and therefore must speak and live so that others will glorify
Him when they hear our message and see our faith in action. —D. J. D.

ONE THING YOU CANNOT DO ABOUT MISSIONS
—ESCAPE YOUR RESPONSIBILITY.

For to me, to live is Christ, and to die is gain.

PHILIPPIANS 1:21

Isaac Asimov tells the story of a rough ocean crossing during which a Mr. Jones became terribly seasick. At an especially rough time, a kind steward patted Jones on the shoulder and said, "I know, sir, that it seems awful. But remember, no one ever died of seasickness." Mr. Jones lifted his green countenance to the steward's concerned face and replied, "Oh, don't say that! It's only the wonderful hope of dying that keeps me alive."

There's more in Jones' words than a touch of irony. As a Christian, I hear echoes of Paul's words to the Philippians. He said that the wonderful hope of dying kept him going (Phil. 1:21–23). Yet he wasn't merely looking for relief from his suffering. Paul's hope was rooted in Christ, who died on the cross for sinners, rose from the grave, ascended to heaven, and would one day take Paul into His presence. The risen Christ is our reason for living.—M. R. D. II

THOSE WHO ARE PREPARED TO DIE ARE MOST PREPARED TO LIVE.

You shall love the Lord your God with all your heart,
with all your soul, and with all your mind.

MATTHEW 22:37

Throughout the London subway system are signs that warn, "Mind The Gap." They remind riders to pay attention to the space between the train and the platform. In the United States I've seen signs along highways with the single word, "Think!" The point of both is clear: In the midst of our daily routine, we often fail to engage our minds in what we're doing.

Could this also happen in our relationship with God? When Jesus was asked to state the greatest commandment, He replied, "You shall love the Lord your God with all your heart, with all your soul, and with all your mind." Our minds are to be as fully yielded to God and as actively engaged in loving Him as our hearts and souls are.

Thinking is hard work, but loving God is a great privilege that deserves all the mental muscle we can put into it. —D. C. M.

TO GROW IN YOUR LOVE FOR GOD, KEEP GOD IN YOUR THOUGHTS.

What God has joined together, let not man separate.

MATTHEW 19:6

*S*ome people would like to leave open the "lock" in wedlock. The vows "for better or for worse . . . till death us do part" sound too risky. One liberal minister said that marriage as we've known it is obsolete. Yet studies show that married people tend to be happier and healthier. A Gallup Poll revealed that 95 percent of Americans consider marriage and family life to be very important to them.

God put a padlock on wedlock because man needed the support and fulfillment that is inherent to a lifelong commitment. In Genesis 2:18, the Lord said, "It is not good that man should be alone; I will make him a helper comparable to him."

God is not only the architect of marriage but also the One who holds it together. —D. J. D.

PUT CHRIST FIRST IF YOU WANT YOUR MARRIAGE TO LAST.

Cast your burden on the LORD, and He shall sustain you.

PSALM 55:22

According to a *Wall Street Journal* report, anxiety has overtaken depression as the leading mental health problem in the United States. Anxiety-fighting drugs are now the top-selling pharmaceutical products.

When David composed Psalm 55, his mind was agitated by the same types of situations we struggle with today: He recoiled in horror from the violence, anger, and abuse that stalked the city streets (vv. 9–11). He suffered the anguish of being betrayed by a close friend (vv. 12–14). He longed to leave and escape to a place of peace (vv. 4–8).

Because David's anxious pain mirrors our own, his prescription for relief can be ours as well. He wrote, "Cast your burden on the LORD, and He shall sustain you." Anxiety is a burden we are not called to bear. —D. C. M.

GOD INVITES US TO BURDEN HIM WITH WHAT BURDENS US.

I will praise You, for I am fearfully and wonderfully made.

PSALM 139:14

Buying a new car is a major investment. We want to be sure we are getting our money's worth. We also want to be certain that the vehicle won't cause us trouble. So we carefully file the manufacturer's warranty, confident that if something doesn't work right we can take our car back to the dealer. Not only are we sure they have trained people who can troubleshoot the problem and fix it, but we know they have all the manufacturer's specifications and the parts that may be needed.

When we run into difficulties in life and aren't able to get things working right, where can we turn for help? Doesn't it make sense that the One who made us is totally qualified to supply the indispensable help we need? The psalmist David found great comfort in this fact. He wrote, "You formed my inward parts; You covered me in my mother's womb. I will praise You, for I am fearfully and wonderfully made; marvelous are Your works . . . . How precious also are Your thoughts to me, O God! How great is the sum of them!" (Ps. 139:13–14, 17). —V. C. G.

GOD'S WARRANTY: YOU'RE COVERED FOR A LIFETIME.

God has chosen the weak things of the world
to put to shame the things which are mighty.

1 CORINTHIANS 1:27

We may say to God, "I am nothing. I have no gifts. I often fail miserably. Do You really want to use me?"

The answer to that question is found in God's Word. He used the hesitant, inarticulate Moses to lead Israel to freedom (Exod. 3:13; 4:10). He used men of the herds and flocks, as well as fishermen and farmers to accomplish His work and record His words. A simple carpenter and a peasant girl raised His Son.

That's still the way God works. Although we have "mega-methods," mass media, and super-churches, it is ordinary people who do God's extraordinary work. God has been using ordinary people for thousands of years. Why would He stop now? —D. C. E.

WANTED: ORDINARY PEOPLE TO DO EXTRAORDINARY WORK.

The testing of your faith produces patience.

JAMES 1:3

Every computer printer shipped by a Colorado company is first frozen, then heated to 130 degrees Fahrenheit, and finally shaken violently for a quarter of an hour. This testing is the final step in a process called "ruggedization," which prepares an ordinary printer for use by the military. With its circuit boards secured and all components enclosed in a metal case, the printer is thoroughly tested to make sure it will work on the battlefield.

If that reminds you of the spiritual "ruggedization" you're undergoing today, take heart. It is God Himself, our loving Father, who allows the times of testing to prepare us to serve Him. When we find ourselves in difficult circumstances, the Bible offers the surprising instruction to "count it all joy . . . , knowing that the testing of your faith produces patience" (James 1:2–3).

As we trust God through the difficult times, we'll become rugged and ready, tested and prepared for greater usefulness. —D. C. M.

**GOD ALLOWS ADVERSITY INTO OUR LIVES
NOT TO BREAK US BUT TO BETTER US.**

There is laid up for me the crown of righteousness,
which the Lord . . . will give to me on that Day.

2 TIMOTHY 4:8

*R*ecently I received a magazine sweepstakes letter that addressed me by name and repeatedly mentioned a $500,000 prize. It spoke of instant wealth and a lifetime of leisure. Finally, at the bottom of page 2, in very small print, I found the part I was looking for. As required by law, the letter told me that the approximate numerical odds of my winning the prize were 1 in 80 million. Now that's remote!

Contrast that with Paul's anticipation of what awaited him in heaven: "There is laid up for me the crown of righteousness, which the Lord, the righteous Judge, will give to me on that Day, and not to me only but also to all who have loved His appearing." Note his assurance: "There is laid up for me." Not "there might be" or "there's a slight chance"—"there is."

If you have welcomed Christ into your life then the same prize awaits you. Count on it, plan on it, anticipate it! It's a promise from God. —D. C. M.

OUR PRESENT CHOICES DETERMINE OUR FUTURE REWARDS.

Without Me you can do nothing.

JOHN 15:5

The Christian life really isn't hard to live—it's impossible! In fact, only one person in history has actually lived it perfectly—Jesus Christ.

The situation isn't hopeless for us, however. When Jesus returned to His Father in heaven, He sent His Holy Spirit to help us live in a supernatural way (John 14:15–17). Just as the Spirit gives us new life in Christ, so also He enables us to live the Christian life as we walk in close fellowship with Jesus (John 15:4–5).

A church bulletin captured this reality in the following prayer: "So far today, Lord, I've done all right. I haven't gossiped; I haven't lost my temper; I haven't been greedy, grumpy, nasty, selfish, or overindulgent. I'm very thankful for that. But in a few moments, Lord, I'm going to get out of bed. And from then on, I'm going to need a lot of help." —H. W. R.

WHAT JESUS ACCOMPLISHED FOR US, THE SPIRIT WORKS OUT IN US.

The Word became flesh and dwelt among us.

JOHN 1:14

A young girl in Africa gave her teacher a Christmas gift. It was a beautiful seashell. "Where did you get this?" the teacher asked. The child told her that such shells were found only on a certain faraway beach.

The teacher was deeply touched, because she knew the girl had walked many miles to find the shell. "You shouldn't have traveled so far just to find a gift for me," she said. The girl smiled and replied, "The long walk is part of the gift."

Jesus Christ gives the wonderful gift of eternal life to all who believe in Him (Rom. 6:23). His gift also began with a journey. He left the splendors of heaven to come to our sin-drenched earth, and walked the long road to the cross. The journey was part of His gift.
—D. C. E.

JESUS GAVE HIMSELF TO GIVE US SALVATION.

Let the word of Christ dwell in you richly.

COLOSSIANS 3:16

Before Clara Schumann, the widow of German composer Robert Schumann (1810–1856), would play any of her husband's music in public, she would first privately read over some of his old love letters. Inspired by his words, she said it seemed as if his very life filled her, and she was then better able to interpret his musical compositions to the public.

In the spiritual realm, if we will read God's words of love to us until we are thrilled by their truth, His Spirit will fill our hearts and minds. We will experience the peace of God.

Spend time in God's Word today so that others will see Christ in your attitudes and actions. —H. G. B.

**WHEN THE WORD OF GOD DWELLS IN YOU,
THE LOVE OF CHRIST SHINES THROUGH YOU.**

*Our light affliction . . . is working for us a far
more exceeding and eternal weight of glory.*

2 CORINTHIANS 4:17

Steinway pianos are built today the same way they were
140 years ago when Henry Steinway started his business.
Two hundred craftsmen and 12,000 parts are required to produce
one of these magnificent instruments. Most crucial is the rim-bending
process, where 18 layers of maple are bent around an iron press to
create the shape of a Steinway grand. Five coats of lacquer are applied
and hand-rubbed to give the piano its outer glow. The instrument then
goes to the Pounder Room, where each key is tested 10,000 times to
ensure quality and durability.

Followers of Jesus Christ are also being "handcrafted." We are
pressed and formed and shaped to make us more like Him. We are
polished, sometimes in the rubbing of affliction, until we "glow." We
are tested in the laboratory of everyday human experience. The
process is not always pleasant, but we can persevere with hope,
knowing that our lives will increasingly reflect the beauty of holiness
to the eternal praise of God. —D. C. E.

TRIALS ARE INTENDED NOT TO PROVOKE US BUT TO PROVE US.

[God] made Him who knew no sin to be sin for us.

2 CORINTHIANS 5:21

Throughout history, royal families have received special treatment. Often they were exempt from keeping the law or receiving punishment or even discipline. But the royal children still needed to know that when they misbehaved they deserved to be punished. When a prince or princess disobeyed or did poorly in schoolwork, the punishment was given to a "whipping boy" instead. There was no doubt who was really at fault, but it was simply unthinkable for a servant to spank a person of royalty.

The cross of Calvary gives a completely different view of dealing with wrongdoing. Although the servant is at fault, royalty receives the punishment. Jesus Christ, the Prince of Glory, took our place when He died on the cross. He voluntarily became our "whipping boy" and paid the penalty for our sins.

How much we owe to Him! —H. W. R.

CHRIST BECAME A CURSE FOR US TO REMOVE THE CURSE FROM US.

If we would judge ourselves, we would not be judged.

1 CORINTHIANS 11:31

State employment officials in Tucson, Arizona, posted an interesting sign over a full-length mirror. Directed to all job hunters, it read, "Would you hire this person?" In another office a mirror and sign posed this question: "Are you ready for a job?"

Self-evaluation was what the apostle Paul called for in 1 Corinthians 11. Believers in Christ need to judge themselves, he said, to avoid being judged by the Lord as unfit for His service. In the Corinthian church, the "appearance problem" was especially serious. Those Christians "looked" awful. They were actually getting drunk and quarreling among themselves while going through the motions of celebrating the Lord's Supper. So Paul said, in effect, "Look at yourselves. What a mess! If you don't get your lives straightened out, the Lord will have to do it for you." Then the apostle added the sobering fact that God had already begun to cleanse the church by sending some of them to an early grave. This is a hard truth, but one the church still needs to hear today. —M. R. D. II

SELF-EXAMINATION IS ONE TEST FROM
WHICH NO CHRISTIAN IS EXCUSED.

Without Me you can do nothing.

JOHN 15:5

When the board members of George Müller's orphanage told him it was impossible to raise enough money to keep the operation going, Müller rejoiced. He said their sense of helplessness would make them rely more fully on the Lord.

Complete dependence on God is an absolute necessity if we are to enjoy His blessing and power. But we seldom learn this truth apart from bitter experience.

Take Jacob, for example. For many years he had lived by his own schemes. Even though distressed when he heard that his brother Esau, whom he had wronged, was coming with 400 men, Jacob had a plan. He tried to make sure that if he were attacked, half of his family would survive. It was then that a "Man" (God in human form) wrestled with Jacob. Just before dawn, the Man demonstrated His deity by putting Jacob's hip out of joint by a mere touch. All Jacob could do was cling to the Man, pleading for His blessing (Gen. 32:26; Hos. 12:4). This was a turning point in Jacob's life, for he learned that blessing comes only from the Lord. —H. V. L.

IF WE DEPEND WHOLLY ON GOD, WE WILL FIND HIM WHOLLY DEPENDABLE.

He who promised is faithful.

HEBREWS 10:23

A young paratrooper admitted that he had been frightened the first time he jumped. There was nothing but a big piece of fabric between him and death. What if that fabric accidentally tore apart? What if his ripcord didn't work and the parachute failed to open?

But when he jumped, everything functioned perfectly. Supported by that life-preserving umbrella over his head, the man floated earthward. He said, "I had a release from fear and a marvelous feeling of exhilaration."

What about the promises God makes in the Bible? Will they uphold us in times of crisis? It all depends on whether we believe them to be God's promises—not merely printed words, black marks on white paper, nor simply the guesses of fallible human beings like ourselves. Because they are the promises of God, we can cling to them with assurance. Throughout the ages He has never been proven untrustworthy. —V. C. G.

TRUSTING GOD'S FAITHFULNESS DISPELS OUR FEARFULNESS.

Cast your burden on the LORD, and He shall sustain you.

PSALM 55:22

*M*y poor computer had gotten overloaded. I had been adding programs to it, storing tons of information, and working on several big projects. Finally it sent me a clear message, informing me that it was incapable of taking any more. If I didn't relieve it immediately, it was going to "crash."

So I got some extra disks and did some quick off-loading. I put each project on a disk of its own and deleted things I didn't need. My grateful computer breathed a sigh of relief.

When we get signals of overload—sleeplessness, irritability, worry—it's time to do some off-loading. It's time to drop some activities and say no to some requests. Above all, as the psalmist suggested, we must off-load our cares on the Lord. He has promised to help us carry our burdens. —D. C. E.

GOD INVITES US TO BURDEN HIM WITH WHATEVER BURDENS US.

They shall still bear fruit in old age.

PSALM 92:14

In his book *The Fisherman and His Friends,* Louis Albert Banks tells about a man who was spending a summer near the shores of Lake Superior. One day he came upon an old pine that had been blown down by a recent storm. Knowing something about trees, he was intrigued by that huge evergreen lying on the ground. He examined it closely and figured that it was at least 250 years old. What impressed him most, however, was what he discovered when he stripped away the bark. It was evident to him that on the day the tree fell it was still growing.

That's the way it should be in the life of a believer. How beautiful are those who grow old gracefully, reflect the loveliness of Christ within their hearts, and keep on being spiritually productive!
—R. W. D.

THE GROWTH OF A SAINT TAKES A LIFETIME.

You greatly rejoice, though now for a little while . . .
you have been grieved by various trials.

1 PETER 1:6

Before passenger trains were equipped with electric lights in their coaches, a Christian man was traveling by rail to a distant city. The route led through several long tunnels. As the man was enjoying a pleasant conversation with the person beside him, the train was suddenly enveloped in total darkness. The other man, also a Christian, had traveled that way many times before. Reassuringly he said, "Cheer up, my friend, we're not in a sack—there's a hole at the other end!"

Frequently, almost without warning, we can pass from the brightness of some great moment with God into a state of gloom and disappointment. Yet God's children are never "in a sack—there's a hole at the other end!" Our "tunnel experiences" are merely the Lord's way of getting us through some mountain we could never scale on our own. —H .G. B.

AT THE END OF THE TUNNEL
GOD'S LOVE SHINES BRIGHTER THAN EVER.

My grace is sufficient for you, for My strength is made perfect in weakness.

2 CORINTHIANS 12:9

dwin Young of Houston, Texas, tells of a man who wanted to buy a Rolls Royce automobile. After several years, he contacted the dealership to determine some pertinent facts about the model he wanted. He learned the price and proceeded with some thorough questions about the vehicle. Only one remained unanswered. "What is the horsepower of this particular engine?" The salesman could not find that information in the brochures. Finally, the sales manager cabled the company in England with the inquiry. The answer came back, just one word, "ADEQUATE."

The apostle Paul's "thorn in the flesh" became the divinely appointed wedge to open his life to the adequacy of God's grace. Though Paul prayed, as we do, to be relieved from the buffeting, he experienced something far greater than freedom from infirmity—grace. No matter the need, the trial, the weakness, God's grace is adequate.

—P. R. V.

GOD'S GRACE KEEPS PACE WITH WHATEVER WE FACE.

[We pray] that you may walk worthy
of the Lord, fully pleasing Him.

COLOSSIANS 1:10

For nearly 5 years my trusty, rusty 1978 Mustang took me back and forth to work. It looked like a refugee from a junkyard, but it ran. I shared the road with some drivers who were "getting there" a bit more fashionably. They rode in brand-new showroom beauties with all the options. They were getting there in style. I was just getting there.

When it comes to how we live on the way to heaven, we all have an opportunity to travel "in style." When we realize all that God has given us in Christ, we shouldn't be content to bump along life's highway like drivers of beat-up old jalopies.

Paul prayed that the believers in Colosse would be "filled with the knowledge of His will in all wisdom and spiritual understanding" (1:9). He wanted them to realize how spiritually rich they were (vv. 12–14). God doesn't want us just to get to heaven. He wants us to enjoy the journey and get there in style. —J. D. B.

KEEP ETERNITY'S GOAL IN SIGHT BY WALKING DAILY IN THE LIGHT.

But let him ask in faith, with no doubting.

JAMES 1:6

Imagine trying to listen to two symphonies at the same time. You turn on two stereo receivers. On one you have Stravinsky's *Firebird Suite,* and on the other, Beethoven's *Ninth Symphony.* Do you listen first to one, then the other? Or do you block out one symphony completely? Or end up with a big headache?

Sometimes we try to live the Christian life that way. In one ear, we hear the voice of God. In the other, we are tuned in to the voice of the world, telling us to make value judgments and solve problems by its standards. But soon we find it impossible to listen to both, and we shut out one of the voices.

Don't give attention to the voice of doubt. Pray in faith. Don't look for answers from another source. Tune in to God only. That's how to avoid hearing double. —D. C. E.

YOU CAN'T TUNE IN ON HEAVEN'S MESSAGE
WHEN YOU'RE PICKING UP EARTHLY STATIC.

As an eagle stirs up its nest, . . . so the LORD alone led him.

DEUTERONOMY 32:11–12

A farmer noticed a bird busily building a nest. Unfortunately, the spot was in a heap of dead branches recently pruned from some trees. Realizing that this was a dangerous place for hatching a brood, the farmer destroyed the nest. The next day, the persistent mother-to-be tried again, and for a second time the farmer thwarted her efforts. On the third day the bird finally began constructing her nest on a limb near the man's kitchen door. This time he let it remain. The unsafe pile of branches from which he had twice driven her was burned long before the bird's eggs were hatched.

We too find that at times our plans are thwarted. We wonder why God would break up the earthly nests we have struggled and worked so hard to build. But were we able to see as He sees, we would know that He seeks for us a higher destiny, a place of greater security and provision for our needs. —H. G. B.

TRIALS TEACH TRUST.

You are great, and do wondrous things; You alone are God.

PSALM 86:10

The king, who liked to be referred to as Louis the Great, had ruled France from 1643 to 1715 with absolute power and incredible splendor. His funeral was held in a magnificent cathedral that was lit by a single candle alongside the ornate coffin. When it was time for Jean-Baptiste Massillon to speak, he reached out and extinguished the flame. Then he broke the silence with the words, "Only God is great."

We recognize and admire some of our fellow mortals who are considered to be great thinkers, great scientists, great inventors, great achievers in every field of endeavor. But they still have the same needs we do. They experience aches and pains. They have troubled minds and hungry hearts. They cannot stave off death or guarantee life beyond the grave.

Only God is truly great—great enough to meet all our needs, great enough to forgive all our sins, and great enough to carry us through the dark valley of death to be with Him forever. —V. C. G.

IN A WORLD OF EMPTY SUPERLATIVES, GOD IS THE GREATEST.

We urge and exhort . . . that you should abound
more and more, . . . to please God.

1 THESSALONIANS 4:1

God is quite popular on Sunday. Millions of people around the world stop what they're doing to visit a building where the sole purpose is to meet with others to worship, sing, and learn about God. But then Monday rolls around. What place does God have in their lives then? When the emphasis is on a thousand other things, they can easily go all week without considering Him.

Where did we get the idea that God wants our attention only on Sunday? Certainly not from the apostle Paul, who said we are to "pray without ceasing" (1 Thess. 5:17)—a sure sign that God is listening on Monday through Saturday too. Paul also wrote, "Rejoice always" (v. 16), which indicates that we shouldn't stop singing just because the organ stops playing.

Sunday is a special day to give direct attention to God. But don't forget Monday! —J. D. B.

WORSHIP GOD ON SUNDAY, THEN WALK WITH HIM ON MONDAY.

[Christ] humbled Himself and became
obedient to the point of death.

PHILIPPIANS 2:8

On July 20, 1969, Apollo 11 astronauts landed on the moon. It was an unprecedented human achievement. Millions remember the words of Neil Armstrong: "That's one small step for man, one giant leap for mankind." President Nixon declared, "All humanity is one in their pride."

Two thousand years earlier, the Creator of the moon made a giant leap of a vastly different kind. He descended from heaven to earth (Phil. 2:5–8). God the Son, (John 1:1, 14), stepped down from heaven to become fully human, while remaining fully God. It was an amazing "leap," which showed us God's heart of love. He became one of us to die on the cross for our sins.

A leap into space may unite mankind in the pride of achievement, but it pales in comparison with what God accomplished when Jesus came from heaven to earth. —D. J. D.

CHRIST WAS BORN HERE BELOW THAT
WE MIGHT BE BORN FROM ABOVE.

I was a stranger and you took Me in.

MATTHEW 25:35

King Abdullah, the ruler of Jordan since 1999, has been known to disguise himself and go out into public places. His purpose is to talk with ordinary people and find out what they are thinking, and to check up on civil servants to see how they are treating his people.

The king got the idea while in New York. He couldn't leave his hotel without being mobbed, so he slipped out in disguise. It worked, so he tried it at home. He reported that once this practice was begun, civil servants and hospital employees started to treat everyone like kings.

When Jesus comes as King, He will judge the nations (Matt. 25:31–46). He said the basis for that judgment will be how people treated Him when He was hungry, thirsty, a stranger, naked, sick, or imprisoned. Those being judged will ask when they saw Him in these situations, and Jesus will say, "Inasmuch as you did it to one of the least of these My brethren, you did it to Me" (v. 40). —D. C. E.

**OUR LOVE FOR CHRIST IS ONLY AS REAL
AS OUR LOVE FOR OUR NEIGHBOR.**

Show me Your ways, O Lord; teach me Your paths.

PSALM 25:4

The Global Positioning System (GPS) is changing the way we work, travel, and play. Using the signals from multiple satellites, an inexpensive GPS receiver can compute your location anywhere in the world. The information can help a lost hiker return to camp, enable a driver to locate a house in a strange city, or guide commercial fishermen to a big catch. In a very real sense, it is "guidance from above."

But it helps only the person who believes the information and acts on it. What good would it be if a person turned off the unit, jammed it in a pocket, and headed out on his own, saying, "I know I'm going east, even if this thing says I'm going south?"

In a similar way, God's guidance through the Bible benefits us only when we trust His Word and obey it. —D. C. M.

GUIDANCE FROM ABOVE IS PROMISED TO ALL WHO FOLLOW GOD'S WORD.

My voice You shall hear in the morning, O LORD.

PSALM 5:3

In an article for the *San Francisco Chronicle*, Herb Caen wrote, "Every morning in Africa, a gazelle wakes up. It knows it must run faster than the fastest lion or it will be killed. Every morning a lion wakes up. It knows it must outrun the slowest gazelle or it will starve to death. It doesn't matter whether you're a lion or a gazelle; when the sun comes up, you'd better be running."

British pastor Charles Spurgeon wrote, "If you are not seeking the Lord, the devil is seeking you." We must not wait until we are attacked by Satan to think about the strategy we should use to escape the enemy of our soul. We must seek the Lord early, keenly aware that "the devil walks about like a roaring lion, seeking whom he may devour" (1 Pet. 5:8). —D. C. E.

PREPAREDNESS = BE READY.

The eyes of the LORD are in every place,
keeping watch on the evil and the good.

PROVERBS 15:3

In this age of electronics, we have all become aware of bugging devices. A person's office, hotel room, or telephone can be monitored so that every sound is picked up. This is accomplished through highly sensitive microphones that are so small they can easily be hidden. Heads of state, government officials, and business people in strategic positions must be exceedingly careful of what they say, especially when entering a strange setting. They must think twice before they speak.

Did you ever stop to think that God sees everything we do and hears everything we say every moment of the day? This truth is both comforting and sobering—comforting because God stands ready to deliver us when we are in trouble (Ps. 33:18–19), and sobering because "the eyes of the LORD are in every place." What a profound effect this should have on the way we live! —R. W. D.

TO KNOW THAT GOD SEES US BRINGS
BOTH CONVICTION AND COMFORT.

LORD, make me to know . . . what is the measure of my days.

PSALM 39:4

The full-page newspaper advertisement for a new car was clever, and it made me think. In bold type it proclaimed that this automobile "goes 0–40 as fast as you did." It went on to say, "What happened? One minute you're studying for mid-terms, then you take a little nap and somehow wake up 20 years later with a job, a mate, and a couple of kids."

It's always a little startling to be confronted with the speed at which our years fly away. Centuries ago, the psalmist David sought God's help as he grappled with the brevity of life. He wrote, "LORD, make me to know my end, and what is the measure of my days." Rather than concluding that nothing really matters because life is so brief, he asked God for deliverance from his sins (v. 8) and for strength to live his remaining days (v. 13).

A popular slogan says, "Life Is Short—Party Hard." But God reminds us, "Life Is Short—Live It Well!" —D. C. M.

**IT'S NOT HOW LONG YOU LIVE THAT
COUNTS, BUT HOW WELL YOU LIVE.**

Let your speech always be with grace.

COLOSSIANS 4:6

The powerful French statesman Richelieu (1585–1642) was also known as a man of great courtesy. On one occasion someone applied to him for a job, knowing that he would be turned down. Richelieu's manner of speech was so warm and accepting that it was worth having a request denied just to hear how graciously he expressed himself—even when he said no. We can all learn from that example.

We as Christians ought to be so sensitive to the needs, hurts, and disappointments of others that no unkind words come from our lips and no harsh tone is heard in our voices—even when we find it necessary to be firm. We have Christ dwelling within us, and as we yield to His control His love will become evident not only in what we say but also in how we say it.

The difference between being an offense or a blessing is sometimes just a manner of speaking. —R. W. D.

GENTLE WORDS FALL LIGHTLY BUT CARRY GREAT WEIGHT.

Blessed are the meek, for they shall inherit the earth.

MATTHEW 5:5

When Jesus said, "Blessed are the meek," He was not advocating a spineless acceptance of life or a doormat mentality. He was telling His followers to be submissive to God and willing to put their strength under His control.

Think of it this way: There is a wonderful cooperation between a powerful horse and its rider. An animal of tremendous size and strength, seven or eight times the weight of a man, submits itself to its master's control. A horse may race, leap, turn, prance, or stand motionless at the rider's slightest command. That's strength under perfect control. And that defines the Christian concept of meekness.

When we willingly place ourselves under the control of God, we are following the example of Jesus Himself while He lived on this earth. He submitted His power to the Father's will (John 5:30; 6:38; Heb. 10:9). —D. C. E.

**IF YOU THINK MEEKNESS IS WEAKNESS,
TRY BEING MEEK FOR A WEEK.**

If the blind leads the blind, both will fall into a ditch.

MATTHEW 15:14

An elderly woman stood on a busy street corner, hesitant to cross because there was no traffic signal. As she waited, a gentleman came up beside her and asked, "May I cross over with you?" Relieved, she thanked him and took his arm.

The path they took was anything but safe. The man seemed to be confused as they dodged traffic and walked in a zig-zag pattern across the street. "You almost got us killed!" the woman exclaimed when they finally reached the curb. "You walk like you're blind!" "I am," he replied. "That's why I asked if I could cross with you."

Jesus said of the Pharisees, "They are blind leaders of the blind. And if the blind leads the blind, both will fall into the ditch" (Matt. 15:14). We have to be careful to entrust our spiritual direction to those who not only walk in the light God's Word but use it to guide others. —P. R. V.

A GOOD LEADER IS ONE WHO SHOWS THE WAY AND GOES THE WAY.

The children of Ephraim . . . forgot His works.

PSALM 78:9, 11

The fine folks of Wilkinsburg, Pennsylvania, had a great idea in 1962. They assembled a time capsule to preserve the town's history for future generations. Then they buried it. The problem was, when they wanted to dig it up in 1987 for a town celebration, no one could recall where it was.

The fine folks of Israel's northern kingdom apparently had a bad case of forgetfulness too, one that affected later generations. But the "children of Ephraim" forgot something far more vital than a steel box full of memorabilia. They forgot the good things God had done for them.

There is always the danger of hiding and forgetting the message of God's love and what He has done for us in Christ. Therefore we must speak often about the works of God to our children. That's how God keeps His truth alive for future generations. —J. D. B.

THE CHARACTER OF OUR CHILDREN TOMORROW
DEPENDS ON WHAT THEY LEARN TODAY.

Lo, I am with you always, even to the end of the age.

MATTHEW 28:20

When the famous missionary David Livingstone made his first trip to Africa, some friends accompanied him to the ship to bid him farewell. They loved him deeply and were greatly concerned for his safety in that far-away land. One of them pleaded with him not to go.

Livingstone, however, was convinced he was doing God's will. Opening his Bible, he read to his friend Jesus' words, "Lo, I am with you always, even to the end of the age." Then he said, "That, my friend, is the word of a gentleman. So let us be going."

Many years later Livingstone was invited to speak at the University of Glasgow. He posed this question to his audience, "Would you like me to tell you what supported me through all the years of exile among a people whose language I could not understand, and whose attitude toward me was always uncertain and often hostile? It was this: 'Lo, I am with you always, even to the end of the age.' On these words I staked everything, and they have never failed." —R .W. D.

HE IS NOT ALONE WHO IS ALONE WITH JESUS.

Do not fear those who kill the body. . . .
Fear him who is able to destroy both soul and body in hell.

MATTHEW 10:28

*S*oldiers have told me that they sometimes experienced great terror during the heat of battle. But they pressed on despite their fear because they were more afraid of what would happen if the enemy was victorious.

A Christian young person who refuses to take drugs with his friends may be afraid they will ridicule him or even hurt him. But he may say no because he is more afraid of suffering the consequences of drug use and of displeasing God.

Jesus said to His disciples, "Do not fear those who kill the body but cannot kill the soul. But rather fear Him who is able to destroy both soul and body in hell." He was not saying that fear of people is wrong. In fact, it is natural, and even beneficial in some instances. What Jesus was saying is that the fear of displeasing God should be our greatest fear. —H. V. L.

THE RIGHT KIND OF FEAR WILL KEEP US FROM DOING WRONG.

Nothing is better for a man than . . .
that his soul should enjoy good in his labor.

ECCLESIASTES 2:24

he 19th-century British author Charles Kingsley wrote,
"Thank God every morning when you get up that you have
something to do that day which must be done whether you like it
or not."

Consider what these three people gave to the world by working
with diligence: Noah Webster labored 36 years and crossed the ocean
twice to produce his dictionary. John Milton rose at 4 o'clock every
morning to compose and rewrite his poetry. Edward Gibbon spent
26 years writing his famous history, *The Decline and Fall of the Roman
Empire.*

What we do may seem insignificant by comparison. But if we
work "heartily, as to the Lord" (Col. 3:23), He will use our labors to
provide for our needs and the needs of others. Any kind of wholesome
work can be a blessing. —H. G. B.

TO LEAVE LASTING FOOTPRINTS ON THE
SANDS OF TIME, WEAR WORK SHOES.

Those members of the body which seem to be weaker are necessary.

1 CORINTHIANS 12:22

A visitor was being shown around a leper colony in India. At noon a gong sounded for the midday meal. People came from all parts of the compound to the dining hall. All at once peals of laughter filled the air. Two young men, one riding on the other's back, were pretending to be a horse and a rider and were having loads of fun.

As the visitor watched, he saw that the man who carried his friend was blind, and the man on his back was lame. The one who could not see used his feet; the one who could not walk used his eyes. Together they helped each other, and they found great joy in doing it.

Imagine a church like that—each member using his or her strength to make up for another's weakness. We need each other. —D. J. D.

THERE IS NO SUCH THING AS INSIGNIFICANT SERVICE FOR CHRIST.

The woman whom You gave to be with me,
she gave me of the tree, and I ate.

GENESIS 3:12

The manager of a minor league baseball team was tired of watching his center fielder play poorly, according to a story by Don McCullough in *Discipleship Journal*. So he grabbed a glove and headed for the outfield to show how it should be done.

The first ball hit toward him took a bad hop and hit the manager in the mouth. Next came a high fly ball that he lost in the sun—only to find it when it smacked him on his forehead. That was enough. Furious, the manager grabbed the center fielder by the uniform and shouted, "You've got center field so messed up, even I can't do a thing with it!"

That may be one of the worst excuses ever given for failing, but we humans have had a lot of practice with alibis. It began with Adam and Eve. When God confronted them about eating the forbidden fruit, Adam blamed God for giving him Eve, and Eve blamed the serpent for giving her bad advice.

Excuses don't hide guilt. When we sin, how much better to admit our failures to both God and man. —J. D. B.

THE SINS WE EXCUSE WILL RETURN TO ACCUSE.

Go into all the world and preach the gospel to every creature.

MARK 16:15

ritz Kreisler (1875–1962), world-famous violinist, earned a fortune from his concerts but he generously gave most of it away. So, when he discovered an exquisite violin on one of his trips, he wasn't able to buy it.

Later, having raised enough money to meet the price, he returned to the seller, hoping to purchase that beautiful instrument. To his great dismay it had been sold to a collector. Kreisler made his way to the new owner's home and offered to buy the violin, but the collector said he would not sell it. Keenly disappointed, Kreisler was about to leave when he asked, "Could I play the instrument once more?" Permission was granted, and the great virtuoso filled the room with heart-moving music. The collector's emotions were deeply stirred. "I have no right to keep that to myself," he exclaimed. "It's yours, Mr. Kreisler. Take it into the world, and let people hear it."

The gospel is like the rapturous harmonies of heaven. We have no right to keep it to ourselves. —V. C. G.

SOMEONE TOLD YOU ABOUT CHRIST. HOW MANY HAVE YOU TOLD?

If you do not forgive men their trespasses,
neither will your Father forgive your trespasses.

MATTHEW 6:15

In World War II, Corrie Ten Boom and her sister Betsie were arrested for concealing Jews and were sent to a German concentration camp. Betsie died a slow and terrible death as a result of the cruel treatment.

Then, in 1947, Corrie spoke about God's forgiveness to a church in Munich. Afterward, a man sought her out. She recognized him as one of the guards who had mistreated her and Betsie. He told her that he had become a Christian, and with extended hand he asked for her forgiveness. Corrie struggled with her feelings, but when she recalled the words of Jesus in Matthew 6:15, she knew she had to forgive. She silently prayed, "Jesus, help me!" and thrust her hand into the hand of her former tormentor.

God asks us to do for others what He has done for us through Jesus Christ. He'll give us strength to forgive. —D. J. D.

SINCE WE ALL NEED FORGIVENESS,
WE SHOULD ALWAYS BE FORGIVING.

I will teach you the fear of the LORD.

PSALM 34:11

We will not get very far in our relationship with God unless we understand that He is to be feared. In *The Chronicles of Narnia,* an allegory by C. S. Lewis, two girls, Susan and Lucy, prepare to meet Aslan the lion, who represents Christ. Two talking animals, Mr. and Mrs. Beaver, prepare the children for the encounter.

"Ooh," said Susan, "I thought he was a man. Is he quite safe? I shall feel rather nervous about meeting a lion."

"That you will, dearie," said Mrs. Beaver. "And make no mistake, if there's anyone who can appear before Aslan without their knees knocking, they're either braver than most or else just silly."

"Then he isn't safe?" said Lucy.

"Safe?" said Mr. Beaver. "Of course he isn't safe. But he's good."

Our holy God isn't "safe," but He is good. —H. W. R.

IF YOU FEAR GOD, YOU NEED FEAR NOTHING ELSE.

*We are . . . pleased rather to be absent from
the body and to be present with the Lord.*

2 CORINTHIANS 5:8

Winston Churchill (1874–1965), former British prime minister, made specific requests regarding his funeral service. He asked that it begin with the playing of "Taps," the traditional military signal played at the end of the day or the end of life. But when Churchill's funeral service was over, those in attendance were startled to hear trumpets play the familiar strains of "Reveille," the stirring call that awakens the troops at the beginning of a new day.

The end of life is in some ways like the end of a day. Life's journey is long. We get tired. We long for our labors to be finished and the suffering to be over. Ahead lies the night of death. But thank God, morning is coming! A wonderful life lies just ahead for the weary Christian traveler. To be absent from the body is to be present with the Lord forever. —D. C. E.

**THE END OF THE CHRISTIAN'S LIFE IS
THE BEGINNING OF A FAR BETTER ONE.**

Let everything that has breath praise the LORD.

PSALM 150:6

What do you do 18 times a minute, 1,080 times an hour, 25,920 times a day, yet rarely notice? The answer: You breathe. If you are 40 years old, you have already taken more than 378 million breaths. And each of those breaths was a measured gift from the hand of God!

Your lungs are among the most important parts of your body. They furnish your blood with oxygen and get rid of carbon dioxide and water. A few minutes without breathing and you would lose consciousness. You could not survive much longer without oxygen.

The Bible tells us that the Lord holds in His hand "the life of every living thing, and the breath of all mankind" (Job 12:10). He gives us those 26,000 gifts each day so that we might honor Him with the life they sustain. —H. G. B.

BREATHE A PRAYER OF THANKS FOR THE BREATH OF LIFE.

These stones shall be for a memorial to the children of Israel forever.

JOSHUA 4:7

In 1941, sculptor Gutzon Borglum completed his work on Mount Rushmore. The 60-foot-high granite heads of four US Presidents now stand like sentinels of democracy over the Black Hills of South Dakota. The imposing likenesses of George Washington, Thomas Jefferson, Abraham Lincoln, and Theodore Roosevelt remind visitors of our nation's heritage and history.

God told Israel's leader, Joshua, to take 12 stones from the middle of the Jordan River for a similar purpose (Josh. 4:1–7, 20–24). The Lord wanted future generations to have a memorial to their national history. He wanted them to remember that as He parted the Red Sea to get them out of Egypt, He also parted the Jordan to get them into the Promised Land. He wanted them to live not only in the present, but with the reminder of the values, faith, and experiences of their founding fathers: Moses, Aaron, and Joshua. We too need to remind one another of God's past provisions.—M. R. D. II

PRECIOUS MEMORIES OF YESTERDAY CAN BE PRECIOUS MOMENTS TODAY.

I have learned in whatever state I am, to be content.

PHILIPPIANS 4:11

A friend in Pennsylvania wrote, "One of my father's old cows gives good milk, but she sure can be dumb! She has a whole field in which to feed, yet no grass seems quite as tasty as those patches outside her own pasture. I often see her stretching her head through the fence, while right behind her is everything she needs—excellent grazing land, beautiful shade trees, a cool, refreshing stream of water, and even a big chunk of salt. What more could she want?"

Many people are like that old cow. They think the "grass is always greener on the other side of the fence." They are constantly grasping, coveting, and seeking to obtain what doesn't belong to them.

If you are a Christian, the greatest blessings in life are already yours. Heaven is your home, and God is your Father. He has promised never to leave you (Heb. 13:5), and He will supply your every need (Phil. 4:19). How green the grass is on your side of the fence! —R. W. D.

**MOST PEOPLE AREN'T CONTENT WITH THEIR LOT—
EVEN WHEN THEY GET A LOT MORE.**

If we confess our sins, He is faithful and just to forgive us our sins.

1 JOHN 1:9

*H*ijackers terrorized the passengers aboard an Indian Airlines jet for 8 days. Then, on December 31, 1999, the gunmen issued a final demand before releasing their hostages. "Sorry, but everyone has to say that I am forgiven," said the hijacker code-named "Burger." When the disbelieving passengers stared back at him, he ordered them to say, "I forgive you." After hearing the words, the hijackers disappeared into the desert.

Not many of us would be so arrogant as to insist that someone forgive us. And we certainly wouldn't demand that of God. Why? Because most people sense that His mercy and pardon can be received only by a humble, sincere, and repentant heart.

None of us is truly free without forgiveness. We need God's, and others need ours. —D. C. M.

CONFESSION IS THE KEY THAT OPENS THE DOOR TO FORGIVENESS.

The Lord Himself will descend from heaven with a shout.

1 THESSALONIANS 4:16

What if everyone had believed the patent office worker who, in 1899, said, "Everything that can be invented has been invented"? Or what if folks in the 19th-century had believed this memo from Western Union: "The telephone has too many short-comings to be seriously considered as a means of communication?"

Predictions about the future are usually bad guesses. When I was a kid, I read science magazines that said that by the end of the 20th century we would all be flying around in air-cars and living in domed houses.

One source for what's ahead, however, is never wrong. It's God's Word! The Bible has reassuring words for those who "believe that Jesus died and rose again" (1 Thess. 4:14). The apostle Paul assures us that "the Lord Himself will descend from heaven with a shout" (v. 16). No matter what's ahead for us, we may with certainty "comfort one another with these words" (v. 18). —J. D. B.

WE CAN TRUST OUR ALL-KNOWING GOD FOR THE UNKNOWN FUTURE.

He gives power to the weak, and to those
who have no might He increases strength.

ISAIAH 40:29

esearchers at the University of Virginia have found that
most people perceive a hill to be steeper than it really is,
especially if they're tired or carrying a heavy load. When asked to
estimate the slope of a hill, test participants consistently misjudged it,
thinking a 10-degree slant was about 30 degrees, and rating a 5-degree
slope as nearly 20 degrees. Hardly any of them believed they could be
that far off.

When we're burdened and exhausted, even a minor problem
can seem too big for us to handle. As we encounter a trial in life, we're
tempted to sit down at the base of that difficult hill and stay there,
convinced that the grade is too steep for us.

That is why we need the encouragement of God's Word. It
draws our attention to our untiring God, who knows our need. In
His strength, we can conquer any difficult hill.—D. C. M.

GOD ALWAYS GIVES ENOUGH STRENGTH FOR THE NEXT STEP.

God resists the proud, but gives grace to the humble.

JAMES 4:6

How did you learn to skate?" someone asked a skating champion. "By getting up every time I fell down," was the reply.

The Christian life is also a series of new beginnings, of falling down and getting up again. When we stumble, we often think, "I've failed again. I might as well give up." But God is the God of new beginnings. He not only forgives our sins, but He also uses our failures to make us wiser.

Sometimes our pride can cause us to resist starting again. In Psalm 25, David showed a heart of humility by praying for forgiveness. He asked the Lord to forgive the sins of his youth (v. 7), and rejoiced that God teaches sinners (v. 8).

Do you feel like a failure? Do you need a new start? Go to the Lord in humility, and He'll show you that He's the God of new beginnings. —J. E. Y.

FAILURE IS NEVER FINAL FOR THOSE WHO BEGIN AGAIN WITH GOD.

You have put gladness in my heart.

PSALM 4:7

David Lykken, Emeritus Professor at the University of Minnesota, has developed what he calls a "set point" theory of happiness. He contends that most people return to their previous level of happiness within 6 months to a year after dramatic events like the sorrow of losing a loved one or the thrill of moving into a dream home. He calls that original reference point of happiness their "set point."

The Christian, however, has a different kind of "set point"—one that does not depend on the normal highs and lows of human experience. The Bible tells us to find our joy and sense of well-being in the unchanging God rather than in our changing circumstances. The psalmist David praised the Lord, saying, "You have put gladness in my heart, more than in the season that their grain and wine increased" (4:7). He had a source of joy that was not tied to economic prosperity.

Let your joy be centered in our unchanging God. —D. C. M.

TO KNOW LASTING HAPPINESS, WE MUST GET TO KNOW JESUS.

A man's pride will bring him low,
but the humble in spirit will retain honor.

PROVERBS 29:23

The story is told of a millionaire who attended a banquet and sat next to some people who were discussing the subject of prayer. He declared, "Prayer may be all right for you, but I don't need it.

I worked hard for everything I have. I didn't ask God for anything!" A university president responded, "Sir, there is one thing you don't have that you might pray for." "And what might that be?" asked the man. The educator replied, "You could pray for humility."

When the Israelites were about to occupy the land of Canaan, Moses looked ahead and knew they would be blessed with an abundance of flocks, silver, and gold—all the result of God's goodness. Knowing that this could easily lead to a feeling of self-sufficiency, he warned that no one should ever boast by saying, "My power and the might of my hand have gained me this wealth" (Deut. 8:17).

Let's honor the Giver of every good and perfect gift (James 1:17) by praising Him for His generosity. —R. W. D.

THE TROUBLE WITH SOME SELF-MADE MEN
IS THAT THEY WORSHIP THEIR CREATOR.

*If we walk in the light as He is in the light,
we have fellowship with one another.*

1 JOHN 1:7

Physical exercise may help us fight off colds and infection. The theory is that a good workout puts our body in a condition similar to what happens at the onset of a fever. Increased body temperature aids our white blood-cell defense system while slowing down the action of bacteria and viruses. Exercise does the same thing. It releases chemicals into the blood that stimulate the brain to make our temperature rise.

The first two chapters of 1 John indicate that a regular practice of good spiritual exercise is beneficial to the health of our soul. To ward off sin, we must "walk in the light as He is in the light" (1:7) and obey Jesus each day.

The right exercise program is one of faith and obedience. It is essential to spiritual health. Walk with Jesus every day, and you'll truly be walking for your health. —M. R. D. II

FOR A HEALTHY HEART, GIVE YOUR FAITH A WORKOUT.

God loves a cheerful giver.

2 CORINTHIANS 9:7

A pastor wanted to see if a farmer in his congregation was willing to support the Lord's work. So one day he challenged him with some direct questions. "If you had two farms," he asked, "would you be willing to give one to God?" "Why, certainly!" replied the man. "I only wish I were in a position to do so."

The minister then asked, "If you had $10,000, would you give $5,000 to the Lord?" Without hesitation the man responded, "How I'd love to have that kind of money! I'd enjoy giving generously like that."

Then the preacher asked: "If you had two pigs, would you give one to the church?" The farmer hesitated for a moment and then blurted out, "That's not fair. You know I've got two pigs!"

Second Corinthians 9:7 tells us not to give "grudgingly or of necessity." As the Lord has prospered us, let's return a portion to Him —wisely, purposefully, and gladly. God loves a cheerful giver! —R. W. D.

**THE HIGHEST KIND OF GIVING COMES
FROM THE BOTTOM OF THE HEART.**

He who sent Me is with Me. . . .
I always do those things that please Him.

JOHN 8:29

John P. Robinson, often called America's "time guru," claims that people today sleep more than they think they do. Though they have more leisure time than ever, they still report feeling "stressed, rushed, and crunched for time."

Robinson calls this problem "overchoice." It's caused by the sheer number of options available to fill our time and the wearying realization that no matter what we choose to do, we are leaving something undone. If our identity is defined by activity, we operate on the principle, "The more we do, the more we are." We are exhausted, and we are the reason.

If Jesus hadn't focused on doing His Father's will, He too could have been overwhelmed by all the demanding tasks He faced. But instead of frenzied activity, Christ personified the focused life in everything He did. He said, "He who sent Me is with Me. The Father has not left Me alone, for I always do those things that please Him" (John 8:29).

—D. C. M.

KEEP FOCUSED ON GOD AND YOU'LL SEE
CLEARLY WHAT HE WANTS YOU TO DO.

Give me understanding, that I may learn Your commandments.

PSALM 119:73

*D*o you believe everything you read in the newspapers? What about the information given on TV news or radio talk shows?

A Roper survey showed that even though Americans overwhelmingly (80 percent) believe that the press is essential to a free society, only 2 percent believe everything a newspaper reporter tells them. For TV news anchors, the trust level is only at 5 percent. And for radio talk-show hosts, that figure drops to 1 percent. Justified or not, it seems that we don't trust our news sources.

There is one news source, however, that will pass the test of 100-percent reliability. It's the biblical record of the good news of Jesus Christ. King David wrote about the reliability of God's Word. In Psalm 19, he called God's law perfect, His testimony sure, and His judgments "true and righteous altogether" (vv. 7, 9). The Bible has news you can trust—and news you can use! —D. C. E.

THE BIBLE: READ IT THROUGH, WORK IT OUT, PASS IT ON!

Blessed are the merciful, for they shall obtain mercy.

MATTHEW 5:7

There's a legend about a rabbi who welcomed a weary traveler into his home for a night of rest. After learning that his guest was almost a hundred years old, the rabbi asked about his religious beliefs. The man replied, "I'm an atheist." Infuriated, the rabbi ordered the man out of his house. Without a word, the elderly man hobbled out into the darkness.

The rabbi was reading the Scriptures when he heard a voice, "Son, why did you throw that old man out?"

"Because he is an atheist, and I cannot endure him overnight!"

The voice replied, "I have endured him for almost a hundred years." The rabbi rushed out, brought the old man back, and treated him with kindness.

God wants us to love unbelievers as He has loved us. His abundant mercy to us is the motivation for us to be merciful to others.
—H. V. L.

**GIVING A PIECE OF YOUR HEART IS BETTER
THAN GIVING A PIECE OF YOUR MIND.**

This grace was given, that I should preach . . .
the unsearchable riches of Christ.

EPHESIANS 3:8

During the Great Depression, a man named Mr. Yates owned a huge piece of land in Texas where he raised sheep. Financial problems had brought him to the brink of bankruptcy. Then an oil company, believing there might be oil on his land, asked for permission to drill.

With nothing to lose, Mr. Yates agreed. Soon, at a shallow depth, the workmen struck the largest oil deposit found at that time on the North American continent. Overnight, Mr. Yates became a billionaire. The amazing thing, though, is that the untapped riches were there all along. He just didn't know it!

Are you a spiritual "Mr. Yates," unaware of the riches you already own in Christ? Paul wrote of "the unsearchable riches of Christ." His goal was to make all Christians see how wealthy they actually are (v. 9). Read Ephesians 3:14–21 and claim your unlimited spiritual treasure today. —J. E. Y.

TO BE RICH IN GOD IS FAR BETTER THAN TO BE RICH IN GOODS.

This hope we have as an anchor of the soul, both sure and steadfast.

HEBREWS 6:19

The president of Gordon College, R. Judson Carlberg, was driving along the ocean near his home in Massachusetts when he saw two stately 17th-century sailing ships. They were replicas, built for a movie being filmed nearby.

"The breeze was stiff," Carlberg reported, "straining the rigging and the crews. Yet each ship stayed the course and didn't capsize." He explained the secret of their stability. "Beneath the waterline each had a deep, heavy keel—a part you don't see." The keel was essential for keeping the vessel steady in rough weather.

What holds us steady when fierce winds are blowing across life's sea? What keeps us from capsizing when we are under stress and tension? It's the stabilizing keel of faith in our sovereign God— the "anchor of the soul." —V. C. G.

CHRIST WILL KEEP US STEADY IN THE STORMY SEA OF CHANGE.

Behold, your King is coming to you . . .
lowly and riding on a donkey.

ZECHARIAH 9:9

Parades have traditionally been celebrations of great achievements. In American history, the greatest parades focused on people such as pilot Charles Lindbergh, the Apollo 11 astronauts, and war heroes. These celebrations were marked by ticker-tape showers and adoring crowds lining the streets of a major city as bands and celebrities passed in review.

But the greatest parade of all time was quite different. It happened in Jerusalem 2,000 years ago. It was a simple one-man donkey ride. Instead of ticker tape, the way was lined with garments and palm branches.

Perhaps the most remarkable element of Jesus' ride into the Holy City was its prophetic significance. In Zechariah 9:9, the prophet described the scene that would unfold more than 500 years later. When Jesus rode that donkey into Jerusalem, fulfilling prophecy as He went, He was giving us one more reason to shout, "Hosanna!" He was, and is, the promised Messiah. —J. D. B.

IF WE BELIEVE IN JESUS' KINGSHIP, WE'LL BOW TO HIM IN WORSHIP.

*[God] does great things past finding
out, yes, wonders without number.*

JOB 9:10

It is God who reminds the sun to rise at its appointed time every morning. It is God who keeps the earth steadily rotating at tremendous speed. It is God who feeds the sparrow and dresses the lilies in their splendor. It is God who guides the feathered flocks southward in the autumn and then brings them north again in the spring.

Argue if you like that all these wonders are simply the operation of the laws of nature. But just as civil law is the expression of human will, so natural law is God's wisdom as it works in keeping with His will.

As we see the wonders of creation all around us, let's worship the One who designed them. —V. C. G.

**WHO SPLASHES RAIN IN SHINING PUDDLES?
THE GOD WHO DESIGNED THEM.**

Though I have all faith . . . but have not love, I am nothing.

1 CORINTHIANS 13:2

A third-grade science teacher asked one of her students to describe salt. "Well, um, it's . . . ," he started, then stopped. He tried again. "Salt is, you know, it's. . ." Finally he said, "Salt is what makes French fries taste bad when you don't sprinkle it on." Many foods are like that—incomplete without a key ingredient. Imagine pizza without cheese, strudel without apples, a banana split without bananas.

The Christian life also has an essential element: love. Paul emphasized its value as he wrote his letter to the Corinthians. Right in the middle of a section about spiritual gifts, he paused to say that even if we have gifts of service, speech, and self-sacrifice but don't have love, we are nothing (1 Cor. 13:1–3).

Doctrinal purity is important. Faith is a magnificent quality, as is obedient service to the Lord. But without love, we're about as bland as French fries without salt. —D. C. E.

AS CHRIST'S LOVE GROWS IN US, HIS LOVE FLOWS THROUGH US.

God, be merciful to me, a sinner!

LUKE 18:13

Charles Haddon Spurgeon used to tell the story of a duke who boarded a galley ship and went below to talk with the criminals manning the oars. He asked several of them what their offenses were. Almost every man claimed he was innocent, blaming someone else or accusing the judge of taking a bribe.

One young fellow, however, replied, "Sir, I deserve to be here. I stole some money. No one is at fault but me. I'm guilty." Upon hearing this, the duke shouted, "You scoundrel, you! What are you doing here with all these honest men? Get out of their company at once!" The duke ordered that this prisoner be released. He was set free, while the rest were left to tug at the oars. The key to this prisoner's freedom was his admission of guilt.

That's also true in salvation. Until a person is willing to admit, "I am a sinner in need of salvation," he cannot experience freedom from guilt and condemnation. —R. W. D.

SIN BRINGS FEAR; CONFESSION BRINGS FREEDOM.

No other foundation can anyone lay
than that . . . which is Jesus Christ.

1 CORINTHIANS 3:11

In 1992, Hurricane Andrew destroyed thousands of homes in South Florida. Yet in an area where the wreckage looked like a war zone, one house remained standing, still firmly anchored to its foundation.

When a reporter asked the homeowner why his house had not been blown away, he replied, "I built this house myself. I also built it according to the Florida state building code. When the code called for 2" x 6" roof trusses, I used 2" x 6" roof trusses. I was told that a house built according to code could withstand a hurricane—and it did."

Jesus said that the person who obeys His Word is like "a wise man who built his house on the rock" (Matt. 7:24). If we build according to His code of obedience, we will not be swept away when crises hit with hurricane-like force. The tempests of temptation and the storms of suffering will not be able to sweep us off a solid foundation of faith and obedience. —V. C. G.

THE STORMS OF OUR LIFE PROVE THE STRENGTH OF OUR FOUNDATION.

Whenever I am afraid, I will trust in You.

PSALM 56:3

A newspaper published the following story from the life of Lyndon B. Johnson, former President of the United States: "In Stonewall, Texas, at a ceremony recognizing highway beautification, the President told his audience he was feeling fine because he had followed the advice of an old woman who once said, 'When I walks, I walks slowly. When I sits, I sits loosely. And when I feels worry comin' on, I just goes to sleep.'"

The expression "When I sits, I sits loosely" caught my attention. It suggests something every believer should be able to do. Those who know Christ and are living in fellowship with Him can experience great blessing and renewed strength by relaxing and trusting God completely. This helps them to avoid getting all uptight. Like the psalmist, they can say with confidence, "Whenever I am afraid, I will trust in You." —R. W. D.

IF YOU GIVE ALL YOUR TROUBLES TO GOD, YOU'LL HAVE NOTHING TO WORRY ABOUT.

Those who worship Him must worship in spirit and truth.

JOHN 4:24

God, the infinitely holy One, is worthy of our worship. He is our Creator, Sustainer, and Savior. Without His loving care and guidance we would have no hope. We must therefore take the time and put forth the effort to worship Him in ways that brings honor and glory to His name.

When Jesus spoke to the Samaritan woman, He said, "God is Spirit, and those who worship Him must worship in spirit and truth." In the devotional classic *The Practice of the Presence of God*, Brother Lawrence explains what this means. "To worship God in truth is to recognize . . . that God is what He is; that is to say, infinitely perfect, infinitely to be adored, infinitely removed from evil, and thus with every attribute divine."

To give almighty God the honor of which He is worthy, we must approach Him "in spirit and truth." —D. C. E.

CHRIST IS NOT VALUED AT ALL UNTIL HE IS VALUED ABOVE ALL.

Run in such a way that you may obtain [the prize].

1 CORINTHIANS 9:24

*I*n the film *Chariots of Fire,* just before the first turn in a 400-meter race, Eric Liddell was shoved off balance and stumbled onto the infield grass. When he looked up, he saw the other racers pulling away. With a look of intense determination, Eric jumped to his feet, and with his back cocked and his arms flailing he rushed ahead. He was determined not only to catch up with the pack but to win. And he did!

This was the kind of fervor the apostle Paul brought to his ministry. In 1 Corinthians 9:24 he said, "Do you not know that those who run in a race all run, but one receives the prize? Run in such a way that you may obtain it." Paul saw himself as an Olympic athlete competing for a gold medal, straining every muscle, nerve, and sinew to get to the finish line. And what's the prize? Not a temporary reward but "an imperishable crown" (v. 25). —H. W. R.

WINNERS NEVER QUIT, AND QUITTERS NEVER WIN.

Abide in Him, that when He appears,
we may have confidence . . . before Him.

1 JOHN 2:28

A school janitor posted a sign in the front schoolyard that read: Keep Off the Grass. But the children still trampled down the turf.

Then a fourth-grade class had an idea. They decided that each child would be given a crocus bulb to plant along the edge of the sidewalk in the fall. As winter drew to a close, the children eagerly watched for the first signs of spring. What a power those hidden bulbs had to keep dozens of little feet on the right path.

We too need a positive motivator to keep our feet on the right path. If our goal is to be able to stand before Christ with confidence and without shame when He comes again, we will want to obey Him (1 John 2:28). As we anticipate that day, and as we become more Christlike right now, we will grow in our confidence. —D. J. D.

JESUS TOOK OUR PLACE THAT WE MIGHT HAVE HIS PEACE.

Blessed is He who comes in the name of the Lord!

MATTHEW 21:9

On that first Palm Sunday, one might have expected Jesus the King to enter Jerusalem on a mighty steed. But He chose instead a lowly donkey. Before He could come as a King to reign, He had to come as a Savior to die. Throughout His life on earth, Jesus was a man of striking contrasts—reflecting both His genuine humanity and His full deity.

Someone has written of Jesus, "He who is the Bread of Life began His ministry hungering. He who is the Water of Life ended His ministry thirsting. Christ hungered as a man, yet fed the hungry as God. He was weary, yet He is our rest. He paid tribute, yet He is the King. He was called a devil, but He cast out demons. He prayed, yet He hears prayer. He wept, and He dries our tears. He was sold for 30 pieces of silver, yet He redeems sinners. He was led as a lamb to the slaughter, yet He is the Good Shepherd. He gave His life, and by dying He destroyed death."—R. W. D.

THE LOWLY CARPENTER OF NAZARETH WAS THE MIGHTY ARCHITECT OF THE UNIVERSE.

Let us run with endurance the race that is set before us.

HEBREWS 12:1

A soccer player knows the importance of perseverance. His opponents will aggravate him, bump him, and knock him down. They try to get him so worried about himself that he can't concentrate on getting the ball into the net. But a good soccer player keeps going for the goal.

That's similar to what we must do when Satan tries to prevent us from living faithfully for Christ. He may use unfair treatment from others or some tempting desire to get us thinking more about ourselves and our needs than about obeying God.

To overcome Satan's strategy, it helps to know that other believers have faced similar circumstances and have finished the race. The "cloud of witnesses" (v. 1) are the saints referred to in chapter 11 who had persevered. Don't get sidetracked as you live the Christian life. Keep going for the goal. —D. C. E.

RUNNING WITH PATIENCE IS PERSEVERANCE IN THE LONG RUN.

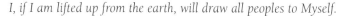

I, if I am lifted up from the earth, will draw all peoples to Myself.

JOHN 12:32

Towering above New York Harbor is the Statue of Liberty. For more than 100 years, that stately lady, with freedom's torch held high, has beckoned millions of people who are choking from the stifling air of tyranny and oppression. They've been drawn to what that monument symbolizes—freedom.

Inscribed on Lady Liberty's pedestal are the deeply moving words by Emma Lazarus: "Give me your tired, your poor, your huddled masses yearning to breathe free, the wretched refuse of your teeming shore. Send these, the homeless, tempest-tossed, to me: I lift my lamp beside the golden door!"

A different monument towers over history, offering spiritual freedom to enslaved people throughout the world. It's the Roman cross where Jesus Christ hung 2,000 years ago. There we see the sinless Son of God dying in our place to pay the penalty for our sins. From the cross we hear the words "Father, forgive them" (Luke 23:34) and "It is finished!" (John 19:30). As we trust in Christ as our Savior, the heavy burden of guilt rolls from our sin-weary souls. We are free for all eternity. —D. J. D.

OUR GREATEST FREEDOM IS FREEDOM FROM SIN.

Be doers of the word, and not hearers only.

JAMES 1:22

A young Christian came into a mission station in Korea to visit the man who had led him to Christ. After the customary greetings, the missionary asked the reason for his coming. "I have been memorizing verses in the Bible," he said, "and I want to quote them to you." He had walked hundreds of miles to recite these verses to his father in the faith.

The missionary listened as he recited without error the entire Sermon on the Mount. He commended the young man for his remarkable feat, then cautioned that he must not only "say" the Scriptures but also practice them. With glowing face, the man responded, "Oh, that is the way I learned them. I tried to memorize them but they wouldn't stick, so I hit on this plan. First, I would learn a verse. Then I would practice what the verse said on a neighbor. After that I found I could remember it."

Could this be the secret of retaining the Word of God? —P. R. V.

TO GET AHOLD OF SCRIPTURE, LET SCRIPTURE GET AHOLD OF YOU.

*Train up a child in the way he should go,
and when he is old he will not depart from it.*

PROVERBS 22:6

A young mother in Kansas made an unusual request of a workman who was smoothing out the freshly poured concrete of a new sidewalk. She asked if she could press her baby's feet onto the concrete. When the man said yes, she stood the child on it and pointed his toes in the direction of a nearby church. Although we don't know what prompted that mother to do this, she apparently wanted to make a permanent impression that would influence the future direction of her little boy's life.

This expression of commitment should reflect the desire of all Christian parents for the spiritual welfare of their children. We must position our young ones on the right way and recognize the importance of the church in their lives. We have the responsibility to encourage them to receive the Lord Jesus Christ as their Savior as soon as they are old enough to understand the meaning of salvation. If we do that, we will cultivate in them a respect for the church and instill in their hearts a love for God and His Word. —R. W. D.

OUR CHILDREN MAY GO WRONG IF WE DON'T START THEM RIGHT.

To Him who is able to keep you from stumbling, . . . be glory.

JUDE 24, 25

A mountain climber in the Alps had come to a treacherous place in his ascent. The only way to advance was to put his foot in the outstretched hands of the guide who had anchored himself a little way ahead of him. The man hesitated a moment as he looked below to where he would certainly fall to his death if anything went wrong. Noticing his hesitation, the guide said, "Have no fear, sir. In all my years of service my hands have never yet lost a man!"

The person who puts the destiny of his soul in Christ's hands can be sure that he will be held securely. Jesus spoke comforting words to His own when He said with divine finality, "They shall never perish" (John 10:28). We are safe not only in His omnipotent hand but also in the Father's eternal grip (John 10:28, 29). —H. G. B.

OUR SALVATION IS SECURE IN GOD'S HANDS.

But You, O LORD, are a shield for me.

PSALM 3:3

*S*ea World in Orlando, Florida, has an underwater shark display that allows you to be in the tank with thousands of pounds of living sharks. A plexiglass corridor makes it possible for you to pass through an aquarium housing scores of them. Guided tours allow you to enter the world of one of man's most feared predators, to sense their presence and power, and yet to be safely shielded from attack.

David had the experience of being in "deep water" surrounded by predators. But as a man after God's own heart he had learned to let the Lord be His protection. What was his secret? According to Psalm 3, David brought his fears to the Lord. He refused to listen to those who said that God would not help him. He even learned to go to sleep, confident that nothing could touch him without the Lord's permission. David found his refuge in God. —M. R. D. II

SAFETY IS NOT THE ABSENCE OF DANGER BUT THE PRESENCE OF GOD.

Then each one's praise will come from God.

1 CORINTHIANS 4:5

According to a legend, a desert wanderer found a crystal spring of unsurpassed freshness. The water was so pure that he decided to bring some to his king. He filled a leather bottle with the water and carried it many days beneath the desert sun to the palace.

When he finally laid his offering at the feet of his sovereign, the water had become stale in the old container. But the king would not let his faithful subject even imagine it was unfit for use. He tasted it with expressions of gratitude and delight, and the loyal man left with a happy heart.

After he had gone, others sampled the water and expressed their surprise that the king had pretended to enjoy it. "Ah," said he, "it was not the water I tasted, but the love that prompted the offering."

Our service may be marked by many imperfections, but the Master looks at our motives. He rejoices in our loyal actions, no matter what others may think. —H. G. B.

WHAT IS DONE FOR CHRIST NOW WILL BE REWARDED IN ETERNITY.

April

I will both lie down in peace, and sleep;
for You alone, O L ORD, make me dwell in safety.

PSALM 4:8

Someone has said, "The rest of your life depends on the rest of your nights." During World War II, an elderly woman in England had endured the nerve-shattering bombings with amazing serenity. When asked to give the secret of her calmness amid the terror and danger, she replied, "Well, every night I say my prayers. And then I remember that God is always watching, so I go peacefully to sleep. After all, there is no need for both of us to stay awake!"

If anxious thoughts keep you awake, ask the Lord to quiet your heart and give you the faith to be able to relax and let Him solve the problems that disturb you. That's what David did when he was in trouble, for he wrote, "I will both lie down in peace, and sleep; for You alone, O L ORD, make me dwell in safety." When you realize your heavenly Father is watching over you, you can find sweet rest. —H. G. B.

BECAUSE GOD NEVER SLEEPS, WE CAN SLEEP IN PEACE.

*Why should it be thought incredible
by you that God raises the dead?*

ACTS 26:8

Resurrection is not an incredible, irrational idea. We can see illustrations of resurrection all around us in nature. For example, Egyptian garden peas that had been buried for 3,000 years were brought out and planted on June 4, 1844. Within a few days they had germinated and broken the ground. Buried for 3,000 years— then resurrected. That's amazing!

Why then should it be thought incredible that God should raise the dead? That was the surprised question of Paul to King Agrippa (Acts 26:8). If God could take some dust and breathe life into it to create a man (Gen. 2:7), why would anyone think it incredible for this same God to raise someone from the dead?

Yes, it is most credible that Jesus would arise. It would be incredible if after the miraculous life He lived He had remained in the grave. Hallelujah! Christ arose! —M. R. D.

ONLY A LIVING SAVIOR COULD RESCUE A DYING WORLD.

Take My yoke upon you and learn from Me,
for I am gentle and lowly in heart.

MATTHEW 11:29

Danish sculptor Bertel Thorwaldsen was commissioned to make a statue of Christ. He first made a model, then left his studio, giving the new-formed clay time to dry and harden. During the night, however, a dense fog rolled in from the sea and the moisture altered the molded figure.

When the sculptor returned the next day, he thought his embryonic masterpiece had been ruined. The hands that had been held aloft as though to bless were now stretched forward in an inviting way. The head of Christ that had been gazing heavenward now looked down toward the earth, partially hiding the face from view.

Looking at the model, Thorwaldsen suddenly realized that this is the way the final sculpture should be formed. "Indeed, if you want to see the face of Christ," he exclaimed, "you must humble yourself and get down on your knees!" —H. G. B.

**THE BEST WAY TO BE "LOWLY IN HEART"
IS WITH A LOVE-FILLED HEART.**

God so loved the world that He gave His only begotten Son.

JOHN 3:16

During World War II it was the custom in the United States for a family who had a son serving in the military to place a star in the front window of their home. A gold star indicated that the son had died in support of his country.

Sir Harry Lauder told a touching story about this custom. He said that one night a man was walking down a New York City street accompanied by his young son. The little fellow was interested in the brightly lighted windows of the houses and wanted to know why some had a star. The father explained that those families had a son fighting in the war. The child would clap his hands as he saw another star in the window and would cry out, "Look, Daddy, there's another family who gave a son for his country."

At last they came to a break in the row of houses. Through the gap a star could be seen shining brightly in the sky. The little lad caught his breath, "Oh, Daddy," he cried, "Look at the star in the window of heaven! God must have given His Son, too." —M. R. D.

**SOME GIVE THEIR LIVES FOR THEIR COUNTRY;
JESUS GAVE HIS FOR THE WORLD.**

He shall be like a tree planted by the rivers of
water, that brings forth its fruit in its season.

PSALM 1:3

Godly men and women are compared in Scripture to
sturdy trees, planted by the rivers of water, laden with fruit,
and full of leaves (Ps. 1:3; 104:16). In order for us to be
fruitful trees, we must:

1. Stand straight for God. Lives that reveal Christlike character are
   lovely to behold, for they are not gnarled by sin or rotted by
   hypocrisy.
2. Be strong. Those who are well-rooted in God's Word will be
   unmovable in times of trial and temptation.
3. Keep growing. As healthy trees add a new ring of growth each
   year, we too should constantly grow in grace (2 Pet. 3:18).
4. Bring blessing to others. Some trees provide food, others give
   shade, and others are made into lumber. So, too, Christians
   should provide spiritual food and comfort to their neighbors and
   use their time and talents to build up others. —H. G. B.

WHEN GROWTH STOPS, DECAY BEGINS.

Others have labored, and you have entered into their labors.

JOHN 4:38

One April morning in the early 1800s John Chapman appeared in Licking Spring, Ohio, staked out a clearing, took some seeds out of a burlap bag that he always carried, and began to plant them. After building a fence around the plot, he departed as quietly as he had come. He then traveled through other towns in Ohio, Indiana, and Michigan, and followed the same procedure.

When Chapman lived in Massachusetts, he had heard that only a few fruit trees existed in the Midwest, so he set out single handedly to remedy the situation. Today this man is known by the name "Johnny Appleseed."

Reflecting on John Chapman's mission, an unknown author has written, "What the world needs are Christians who will be 'spiritual Johnny Appleseeds,' because men and women all around us are dying in sin. The Word of God is the seed that will give them life—food for their souls, gain for eternity, and beauty for ashes." —H. G. B.

WE PLANT THE SEED; GOD GIVES THE HARVEST.

The LORD preserves all who love Him.

PSALM 145:20

A young girl traveling on a train for the first time heard that it would have to cross several rivers. She was troubled and fearful as she thought of the water. But each time the train came near to a river, a bridge was always there to provide a safe way across.

After passing safely over several rivers and streams, the girl settled back in her seat with a sigh of relief. Then she turned to her mother and said, "I'm not worried anymore. Somebody has put bridges for us all the way!"

When we come to the deep rivers of trial and the streams of sorrow, we too will find that God in His grace "has put bridges for us all the way." So we need not fall into hopelessness and anxiety. He will provide for us and carry us through the difficulties to the other side. Instead of worrying about what's ahead, we can trust the Lord to be there to care for us. —H. G. B.

WHERE GOD GUIDES, HE PROVIDES.

Whom He foreknew, He also predestined
to be conformed to the image of His Son.

ROMANS 8:29

Someone has said that the Father was so pleased with His Son that He has determined to fill all of heaven with others just like Him.

When Jesus returns, "we shall be like Him" (1 John 3:2), but the process of becoming like Him begins here and now. How does that happen? It is explained by the "all things" of "all things work together for good to those who love God" (Rom. 8:28). This includes testing and trials, chastening and suffering. To become like Him, we must follow Him, and that is the path of sacrifice and submission (Heb. 2:10).

Following Jesus means we must be willing to go with Him to the Garden of Gethsemane and up the hill of Calvary. We must be willing to endure suffering and rejection by those who reject Him (John 15:18–21). But following Him also leads us to the empty tomb and the place at the right hand of God. "If we endure, we shall also reign with Him" (2 Tim. 2:12). —M. R. D.

AS YOU WALK WITH HIM, YOU WILL GROW TO BE LIKE HIM.

Though I walk through the valley of the shadow of death, I will fear no evil; for You are with me.

PSALM 23:4

Author William H. Ridgeway recalls that when he was a boy he and his friends would pick berries. After filling their baskets, they would wait beside a nearby railroad track. As the sun was sinking in the west, a train would come by and "run over them." Of course the iron monster with its thundering noise and screaming whistle didn't actually run over them at all. It was only the shadow that passed over them.

There they sat, knowing there was no danger but shivering in anticipation at the approaching locomotive and boxcars. As the train swept by them, they were in its shadow for just a few moments and then it was gone. The setting sun bathed them in a golden glow as they walked to the inviting warmth of home. What a wonderful illustration of what it means for the Christian to "walk through the valley of the shadow of death."

We need not fear the shadow of death for the Lord will walk us all the way home (2 Cor. 5:1–8). —H. G. B.

FOR THE CHRISTIAN, DEATH IS THE LAST SHADOW BEFORE HEAVEN'S DAWN.

For this cause I have come into the world.

JOHN 18:37

G od has a plan for our lives that is complete in every
detail. The Sovereign of the universe cannot allow any of
His plans to be executed haphazardly. He leaves nothing to
happenstance.

The life of Jesus is a prime example. His coming as a Babe
in Bethlehem, His earthly ministry, His death, and His resurrection
all took place according to God's purpose. To show that Jesus was
determined to do His Father's will, Luke wrote, "He steadfastly set
His face to go to Jerusalem" (Luke 9:51). Jesus' death was no turn
of fate—it was a fulfillment of God's plan. He came to give His life
a ransom for the sins of the world.

It is also true that the life of every Christian has been designed by
God to fulfill a specific purpose. C. H. Spurgeon said, "There is not a
spider hanging on the king's wall but has its errand; there is not a nettle
that grows in the corner of the churchyard but has its purpose. . . . And
I will never have it that God created any man to be a nothing." —P. V.

DUTIES BELONG TO US; RESULTS BELONG TO GOD.

Walk in wisdom, . . . redeeming the time.

COLOSSIANS 4:5

uthor and lecturer John Erskine (1879–1951) declared that he learned the most valuable lesson of his life when he was 14 years old. His piano teacher asked him how much he practiced. He replied that he usually sat at the instrument for an hour or more at a time.

"Don't do that," warned the teacher. "When you grow up, time won't come to you in long stretches like that. Practice in minutes wherever you can find them—5 or 10 before school, a few after lunch. Sandwich them in between chores. Spread the practice throughout the day, and music will become a part of your life."

Erskine stated later that by following this advice he was able to live a fulfilled life as a creative writer, in addition to his regular duties as an instructor. He wrote nearly all of *Helen of Troy,* his most famous work, on streetcars while commuting between his home and the university.

Use your spare moments to read the Bible, or to pray, or to write a note of encouragement to a needy soul. —H. G. B.

WASTING TIME INSULTS THE GIVER OF TIME.

Do not worry about tomorrow . . . .
Sufficient for the day is its own trouble.

MATTHEW 6:34

I once read about a paratrooper in the US Army who had made more than 50 successful parachute jumps without a single serious injury. But the first day back home after being discharged, he stumbled over a rug, fell against a table, and broke four of his ribs! He had worried a great deal about his parachute jumps, but then something happened he had never worried about: He tripped over a rug.

So why worry? Jesus said that it's futile to fret, for worrying can't change anything (Matt. 6:27). We need to remember that our heavenly Father knows all about our situation and watches over us. He will take care of our needs no matter what tomorrow brings.

Remember, worry never solved a single thing! —M. R. D.

**WORRY DOESN'T IMPROVE THE FUTURE,
IT ONLY RUINS THE PRESENT.**

He was wounded for our transgressions,
He was bruised for our iniquities.

ISAIAH 53:5

When you study the painting of the crucifixion by the famous Dutch artist Rembrandt, your attention is first drawn to the cross and to Jesus. Then, as you look at the crowd around the cross, you are drawn to the faces of the people involved in the awful crime of crucifying the Son of God. Finally, your eyes drift to the edge of the picture and catch sight of another figure—almost hidden in the shadows. This, we are told, was a self-portrait of Rembrandt, for he recognized that by his sins he helped nail Jesus there!

Someone has aptly said, "It is a simple thing to say that Christ died for the sin of the world. It is quite another thing to say that Christ died for my sin!"

Think again of Rembrandt's painting. If you look closely, you will see that in the shadows you, too, are standing. Christ bore the penalty of your sin. He was wounded for you. —H. G. B.

CALVARY REVEALS MAN'S HATRED FOR
GOD AND GOD'S LOVE FOR MAN.

Where were you when I laid the foundations of the earth?

JOB 38:4

Joe and Charlie were arguing about Genesis 1:1. Joe said he believed the record of creation just as it was written. Charlie was an unbeliever, and went to great lengths in giving his own theory of how the world began and then how life developed from a primordial cell through reptiles, monkeys, and up to man. When he was all through, Joe looked at him and said, "Were you there, Charlie?" It was a good question. "Of course I wasn't there," he replied. Joe said, "Well, God was. He was the only one there and I'll take the word of the Eyewitness rather than the guesses of those who rely on their own imagination."

In a court of law, eyewitness testimony carries the most weight. Hearsay testimony is thrown out. The same is true of creation. God asked Job the question, "Where were you when I laid the foundations of the earth?" (Job 38:4). God was there, and His Word can be trusted. —M. R. D.

YOU WILL TRUST THE BIBLE WHEN YOU TRUST ITS AUTHOR.

Happy are the people whose God is the LORD!

PSALM 144:15

When W. B. Davidson was a young boy, he walked with his father three miles from his rural home to his grandmother's house. While they were visiting, the sun set. Davidson writes, "Between our home and grandmother's house was a swamp. That night the croaking of the frogs, the chirping of the crickets, and the shadows of the trees frightened me. I asked my father if there was any danger of something catching us, but he assured me that there was nothing to dread. And so, taking me by the hand, he said, 'I will not allow anything to harm you.' Immediately my fears passed away and I was ready to face the world."

Someone has said that the three keys to real peace are: fret not, faint not, fear not.

1. Fret not—because God loves you (1 John 4:16).

2. Faint not—because God holds you (Ps. 139:10).

3. Fear not—because God keeps you (Ps. 121:5).

God holds our hand. We have nothing to fear. —H. G. B.

THE PERFECT ANTIDOTE FOR FEAR IS TRUST IN GOD.

The people had a mind to work.

NEHEMIAH 4:6

When Deborah, Israel's fourth judge, sang her song in celebration of Israel's victory over the Canaanites (Judges 5:2–31), she mentioned the tribe of Reuben. They had "great resolves of heart," but were content to sit "among the sheepfolds."

The tribe of Reuben was like the boy who sat at his mother's desk, carefully drawing a picture. Soon he laid down his pen and proudly showed his mother his sketch of the family dog. She commented on the fine likeness, then noticed that something was missing. "Where is Rover's tail?" she asked. "It's still in the bottle," the boy explained.

Many important things in the Christian life are left undone because we don't put our plans into action. No matter how good our intentions, they can't glorify God if they are "still in the bottle." —P. R. V.

WE MAY BE ON THE RIGHT TRACK, BUT WE WON'T GET ANYWHERE IF WE JUST SIT THERE.

*Be vigilant; because your adversary the devil walks
about like a roaring lion, seeking whom he may devour.*

1 PETER 5:8

A man was repeatedly robbed by burglars who entered his house through a window while he was asleep. He finally solved his problem by using three things. He called them a twinkler, a tinkler, and a tattler. The twinkler was a candle that he kept burning in the window all night. The tinkler was a bell attached to the window. And the tattler was a small, noisy dog. Because of these, the burglars were kept away.

Every Christian lives in a house that Satan seeks to burglarize. We too need a twinkler, a tinkler, and a tattler. The twinkler is the candle of God's Word. Its truths provide light that exposes Satan's lies. Daily attention to the Word keeps the lamp bright. The tinkler is the bell of our testimony. Keep it ringing as you tell others of the Savior, and Satan will be frustrated. The tattler is the life of prayer. When the enemy comes, send up the warning that you are telling Jesus about it all. Yes, twinkle your light, tinkle your testimony, and bark the enemy away by prayer. —M. R. D.

IF YOU WOULD MASTER TEMPTATION, LET CHRIST MASTER YOU.

His name will be called Wonderful, Counselor, . . . Prince of Peace.

ISAIAH 9:6

When Jesus rode into Jerusalem on a donkey, the crowds cried out, "Hosanna to the Son of David!" (Matt. 21:9). Later that same week, however, a mob called for His crucifixion (27:22). Few people recognized Him as the one Isaiah described as Wonderful (Isa. 9:6).

If there is anyone who deserves that name, it is Jesus. He is wonderful in His deity and in His selfless love that led Him from the shining glories of heaven into the darkness of this sin-cursed world. He is wonderful in His virgin birth, wonderful in His overcoming, sinless life of service, wonderful in His teachings, wonderful in His vicarious death, wonderful in His astounding resurrection, and wonderful in His ascended glory.

Someone has observed, "In Christ we have a love that can never be fathomed, a peace that can never be understood, a rest that can never be disturbed, a joy that can never be diminished, a hope that can never be disappointed, and a spiritual resource that can never be exhausted." —H. G. B.

THE VICTIM OF CALVARY BECAME THE VICTOR OF EASTER.

As far as the east is from the west, so far has
He removed our transgressions from us.

PSALM 103:12

How far is the east from the west? If I were in New York and wanted to travel as far west as possible, how far would I have to go? When I reach Los Angeles, the Philippines are still west, and after that China is still west, and from there Europe is west, and from Europe I go back to New York.

How far west must I go to reach the east? It cannot be measured.

Someone asked an elderly Christian, "Does the devil ever trouble you about your past sins?" She answered, "Yes." When asked what she does then, she replied, "Oh, I just tell him to go east." "What do you do if he comes back?" "I tell him to go west." "And when he comes back from the west, what do you do then?" She said, "I just keep him going from the east to the west." —M. R. D.

WHEN GOD SAVES US, OUR SINS ARE
FORGIVEN AND FORGOTTEN FOREVER.

Do not despise the chastening of the LORD.

PROVERBS 3:11

Scientists tell us that the seeds of certain types of desert bushes must be damaged by a storm before they will germinate. Covered by hard shells that keep out water, these seeds can lie dormant on the sand for several seasons until conditions are right for growth. When heavy rains finally bring flash floods, the little seeds are banged against sand, gravel, and rocks as they rush down the slopes. Eventually they settle in a depression where the soil is damp. Able to absorb water through the nicks and scratches they acquired on their downhill plunge, they finally begin to grow.

Sometimes Christians are like those seeds. We need bad weather to stimulate our spiritual development. Although the heavenly Father never allows His children to suffer needlessly, sometimes He lets us experience nicks and scratches that let the water of His word seep in and soften our hearts. —M. R. D. II

**WE MAY PREFER TO REMAIN SEEDS,
BUT GOD WANTS US TO BECOME TREES.**

God forbid that I should boast except in the cross of our Lord Jesus Christ, by whom the world has been crucified to me, and I to the world.

GALATIANS 6:14

A woman rushed up to violinist Fritz Kreisler after a concert and gushed, "Oh, I would give my life to play as you do!" He answered soberly, "That's exactly what I did."

Kreisler had made a great sacrifice of time, effort, and personal desires to attain such accomplishment. So, too, in the spiritual realm, if we would become mature followers of Christ, we must be willing to die to self.

Three crucifixions are in view in Galatians 6:14. First is the crucifixion of Christ. His sacrificial death on the cross provided our salvation. Second is the crucifixion of the world. Its pleasures, honors, treasures, must be rejected. Third, we as believers are crucified, no longer responsive to the world's temptations. The first cross speaks of the basis of our salvation, the second deals with the result of our salvation, and the third points to the living out of that salvation from day to day. —H. G. B.

CHRIST DIED FOR SIN SO WE COULD DIE TO SELF AND SINFUL PLEASURES.

Serve the LORD with fear, and rejoice with trembling.

PSALM 2:11

The caretaker of the home where Beethoven spent his final years led a group of tourists to the room that housed a stately old piano. Lifting the cover with an air of reverence, he said, "This was Beethoven's piano!" A young woman stepped forward, sat down on the music stool, and began playing one of Beethoven's sonatas. Concluding, she spun around and said to the shocked caretaker, "I suppose many people who visit here like to play Beethoven's piano." "Well, Miss" he replied, "last summer the world famous Paderewski was here, and some of his friends wanted him to play, but he said, 'No, I am not worthy.'"

After a glimpse of God's holiness, Isaiah cried out, "Woe is me!" (Isa. 6:5). And John the Baptist said of the Messiah, "He who is coming after me is mightier than I, whose sandals I am not worthy to carry." A healthy sense of our unworthiness before God makes us rely more than ever on the worthiness of Jesus. That's the secret of becoming like Him. —D. J. D.

TRUE WORSHIP ACKNOWLEDGES THE TRUE WORTH-SHIP OF GOD.

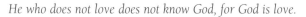
He who does not love does not know God, for God is love.

1 JOHN 4:8

A farmer placed a weather vane inscribed with the words "God is love" on top of his barn. One day a traveler stopped by the farm and watched the weather vane moving with the breeze. Then, with a smirk on his face, he asked, "Do you mean to say that your God is as changeable as the wind?"

The farmer shook his head and replied, "No. What I mean to say is that no matter which way the wind blows, God is love!"

The statement "God is love" implies much more than that God demonstrates His love regardless of the circumstances. It means that love is the essence of God's character. We will never be able to plumb the depths of His love—not even in eternity. But the apostle John pointed out that we can begin to understand it as we view the cross (1 John 4:9–10). As we see Christ dying there for us, we catch a glimpse of the beauty of the loving heart of God. —H. G. B.

A PERSON WHO KNOWS GOD'S LOVE SHOWS GOD'S LOVE.

Thanks be to God for His indescribable gift!

2 CORINTHIANS 9:15

It has been said that one of the Roman emperors gave an expensive present to a friend. But when the ruler offered the gift, the friend said, "This is too much for me to receive." The emperor replied, "But it is not too much for me to give."

When we think about all our sinfulness and rebellion, God's "indescribable gift" (2 Cor. 9:15) of forgiveness through Jesus Christ seems too much for us poor sinners to receive. God is so rich in mercy, though, that it is not too much for Him to give.

Who can estimate the preciousness of God's gift of salvation through His Son the Lord Jesus? All we can do now and throughout eternity is to fall down in adoration before the Lord, praising Him for a salvation so wondrous and so free! —H. G. B.

PRAISE IS THE LANGUAGE OF A HEART SET FREE.

Keep yourself pure.

1 TIMOTHY 5:22

A writer who visited a coal mine noticed a perfectly white plant growing by the side of the entrance. He was astonished that there, where coal dust continually blew and settled, this little plant would be so pure and white. As the author watched, a miner took some black coal dust and threw it on the plant, but not a particle stuck. Nothing could stain the plant's snowy whiteness.

Enoch lived in the days before the flood, a time when "the LORD saw that the wickedness of man was great in the earth, and that every intent of the thoughts of his heart was only evil continually" (Gen. 6:5). Yet the Bible tells us that "Enoch walked with God three hundred years" (5:22).

It is our mission to be pure and unspotted from the ungodly influences in the world. How is this possible? If the Lord can keep a plant white as snow amid clouds of black dust, can He not by His grace keep your heart pure in this world of sin? —M. R. D.

WE LIVE IN THE WORLD, BUT THE WORLD MUST NOT LIVE IN US.

Attend to my cry, for I am brought very low.

PSALM 142:6

According to a legend, a king once placed a heavy stone in the roadway. Then he hid and waited to see who would remove it. Many who came by loudly blamed the government for not keeping the highways clear, but none assumed the duty of pushing the obstacle out of the way. At last a poor peasant stopped and rolled it into the gutter. To his surprise he found a bag full of gold embedded in the road beneath the spot where the rock had been. A note said it was the king's reward for anyone who removed the troublesome object.

So too, our King has hidden a blessing under every trial. The obstacles on our path are placed there for a purpose. By them God tests our faithfulness, turns our attention heavenward, and gives us opportunity for spiritual reward. —H. G. B.

NO TRIAL IS WITHOUT GOD'S BLESSING.

Your word is a lamp to my feet, and a light to my path.

PSALM 119:105

If you have ever carried a lantern on a dark road at night, you know that you cannot see more than one step ahead of you. But as you take that one step, the lamp moves forward, making the next step plain. You reach your destination safely without once walking in darkness. You have light the entire way, even though it is only enough for one step at a time.

The writer of Proverbs said, "Trust in the LORD with all your heart. . . . In all your ways acknowledge Him, and He shall direct your paths" (Prov. 3:5–6). As we refuse to worry about the "tomorrows" and begin to trust God for the "todays," we find grace and guidance for each step of the way. We don't need to see beyond what God shows us today. When we follow His leading, we have enough light for each step of the way. —R. W. D.

THE LANTERN OF GOD'S TRUTH WILL GUIDE YOU IN THE NIGHT.

Do all things without complaining.

PHILIPPIANS 2:14

During the years I was a medical doctor, I had a number of patients who seemed to enjoy complaining about their physical ills. I would examine them and not find a single thing wrong, yet all they did was whine and complain. Pains here, aches there, and as one expressed it, "I just feel no good all over." In my opinion, it was all imaginary. It seemed to me that if they would only start to count their blessings they would soon forget their troubles.

How different the case of the very old woman, penniless and weak, who was asked, "Auntie, how is your health?" "Oh, I have so much to be thankful for," she replied. "I have only two teeth left, but thank God, they are opposite each other!"

Before you begin another day, stop to count your blessings instead of dwelling on your troubles. —M. R. D.

INSTEAD OF COMPLAINING, COUNT YOUR BLESSINGS.

Whoever desires to be first among you, let him be your slave.

MATTHEW 20:27

Jean Frederic Oberlin, a minister in 18th-century Germany, was traveling by foot in winter when he was caught in a severe snowstorm. He soon lost his way in the blowing snow and feared he would freeze to death. In despair he sat down, not knowing which way to turn. Just then, a man came along in a wagon and rescued Oberlin. He took him to the next village and made sure he would be cared for.

As the man prepared to journey on, Oberlin said, "Tell me your name so that I may at least have you in grateful remembrance before God." The man, who by now had recognized Oberlin, replied, "You are a minister. Please tell me the name of the Good Samaritan." Oberlin said, "I cannot do that, for it is not given in the Scriptures." His benefactor responded, "Until you can tell me his name, please permit me to withhold mine."

Jesus did not come to be praised and served, but to serve others unselfishly. —P. R. V.

**WHEN WE FORGET ABOUT OURSELVES,
WE DO THINGS OTHERS WILL REMEMBER.**

Let heaven and earth praise Him,
the seas and everything that moves in them.

PSALM 69:34

What animal is longer than 3 dump trucks, heavier than 110 Honda Civics, and has a heart the size of a Volkswagen Beetle? The answer is a blue whale. How much food does it take to sustain such an animal? Try 4 tons of krill a day—that's 3 million calories! Even a baby blue whale can put away 100 gallons of milk every 24 hours. When a blue whale surfaces, it takes in the largest breath of air of any living thing on the planet. Its spray shoots higher into the air than the height of a telephone pole.

The hand of God gives life and breath to every creature; animals, birds, and fish all speak of His wisdom and power (Job 12:7–10). That is certainly true of the blue whale. Its enormous size and strength call for vast supplies of food—resources provided by the Lord when He created it.

Did the blue whale come into existence by chance? By some evolutionary quirk? No way! —D. C. E.

ALL CREATION IS AN OUTSTRETCHED FINGER POINTING TOWARD GOD.

You are the God of my salvation; on You I wait all the day.

PSALM 25:5

What can ride ocean currents for years before finally washing ashore and springing to life? According to National Geographic's *World* magazine, it's a nut, native to South America and the West Indies. Some people call them "sea hearts."

These 2-inch, chestnut-colored nuts are hardy, heart-shaped seeds that grow on high-climbing vines. They often fall into rivers and float out to sea. There they may ride the currents for years before coming to shore and sprouting into a plant.

This life-bearing, wave-riding seed reminds me of a basic spiritual principle. God's plans may include extended times of waiting for Him to act on our behalf. This was true of Noah, who endured ridicule while spending 120 years building a ship, and of Abraham, who waited for the fulfillment of God's promise that he would have a son in his old age.

Nothing is harder or better for us than waiting on the Lord.

—M. R. D. II

GOD MAY STRETCH YOUR PATIENCE TO ENLARGE YOUR SOUL.

*Teach me, O LORD, the way of Your statutes,
and I shall keep it to the end.*

PSALM 119:33

A Scottish shepherd stood waving his arms on the lush, green hillside. His flock had broken away and was straying across the road while motorists honked, further adding to the sheep's bewilderment. From the top of the slope, the shepherd tried in vain to direct his faithful sheepdog. But the chaos of horns blowing and the distance from the shepherd made it impossible for the dog to get his master's instructions. He was distracted.

Finally, in desperation, the dog dashed up the hill to his master, leaving the confusion below. Standing quietly at the shepherd's feet, the dog's eyes and ears took in the commands. Then down he ran, this time knowing exactly what to do. Soon he had gathered the sheep and steered them away from the road.

As followers of Christ, how quickly we can lose our sense of direction because of the world's distractions! Time alone with Him and His Word will clear our hearts and minds to understand His will.

—P. R. V.

TO HEAR GOD'S VOICE, TURN DOWN THE WORLD'S VOLUME.

Through [Christ] we have now received the reconciliation.

ROMANS 5:11

Veteran missionary pilot Bob Griffin tells about the difficulty Bible translators had putting the word *reconciled* into the native Auca language. They searched for an equivalent but found none. Then one day a translator was traveling through the jungle with some of the Auca people. They came to a narrow, deep ravine, and the missionary thought they could go no farther. The Aucas, however, took out their machetes and cut down a large tree so that it fell over the ravine, permitting them all to cross safely.

The translator, listening intently to the Aucas, discovered that they had a word for "tree across the ravine." This seemed to be the best way to express the meaning of the word *reconciled*.

The great "ravine" between sinful man and a holy God was bridged by Jesus Christ. He became man, lived a sinless life, and died for us. He reconciled us to God. He is our "tree across the ravine."
—D. C. E.

CHRIST WAS DELIVERED FOR OUR SINS THAT
WE MIGHT BE DELIVERED FROM OUR SINS.

Examine me, O Lord, . . . try my mind and my heart.

PSALM 26:2

A teenager by the name of Jimmy stopped at a neighborhood store and asked if he could use the telephone. Given permission, he proceeded to make his call.

The conversation went something like this: "Hello. Is this Mr. Brown? I was wondering whether you needed anyone to cut your grass. Oh, you already have someone? Is he doing a good job? He is? Are you sure you don't want to hire someone else? You're positive? All right, then. Thank you. Good-by."

As the boy hung up, the owner of the store, who had overheard what he said, commented, "I'm sorry, Jimmy, that you didn't get that job." "Oh, don't worry about that," answered Jimmy. "I already work for Mr. Brown. I was just checking up on myself."

As believers in Christ, we too should check up on ourselves regularly. We should invite Him to examine every area of our lives.
—R. W. D.

DETECTING SIN IS THE FIRST STEP IN DELIVERANCE FROM SIN.

Rejoice because your names are written in heaven.

LUKE 10:20

At one time Frederick the Great held a banquet at which Voltaire, the French philosopher and skeptic, was present. When dinner was served, the noted unbeliever began to ridicule the Christians who were there. Finally he said, "Why, I would sell my seat in heaven for a Prussian dollar!"

There was a pause. Then one of the guests quietly rose from his chair and said, "Sir, you are in Prussia, where we have a law which requires that one who wishes to sell anything must first prove ownership. Are you prepared to establish the fact that you have a seat in heaven?" Surprised and embarrassed, Voltaire, the normally quick-witted scoffer, had nothing more to say for the rest of the evening.

How different with those of us who have been joined to Christ through faith! We are sure of a place in heaven. —H. G. B.

WHEN WE RECEIVE CHRIST, WE BECOME STOCKHOLDERS IN HEAVEN.

Do not be afraid, but speak and do not keep silent.

ACTS 18:9

*A*re you discouraged because the work that God has called you to do is off to a slow start? Remember, some of our most wonderful inventions got off to slow starts as well.

The first electric light was so dim a candle was needed to see its socket. The first steamboat took 32 hours to chug its way from Buffalo to Albany, a distance of 522 miles. Wilbur and Orville Wright's first airplane flight lasted only 12 seconds.

In his ministry at Corinth, the apostle Paul went every Sabbath to the synagogue and tried to persuade the Jews that Jesus is the Christ, but they refused his message. So he turned to the Gentiles, and many believed.

Don't let a rough beginning in your endeavor for the Lord get you down. When you know you're in God's will, stick with it!

—D. C. E.

GOD CAN MAKE A GREAT FINISH OUT OF A SLOW START.

Honor your . . . mother, as the LORD
your God has commanded you.

DEUTERONOMY 5:16

A teacher gave her class of second-graders a lesson on the magnet and what it does. The next day, in a written test, she included this question: "My name has six letters. The first one is m. I pick up things. What am I?" When the test papers were turned in, the teacher was astonished to find that almost 50 percent of the students answered the question with the word mother.

Yes, mothers do pick up things. But they are much more than "magnets," gathering up clothes and picking up toys around the house. As willing as many mothers are to do such chores, they have a higher calling than that.

A good mother loves her family and provides an atmosphere where each member can find acceptance, security, and understanding. She is there when the children need a listening ear, a comforting word, a warm hug, or a loving touch on a fevered brow. And for the Christian mother, her greatest joy is in teaching her children to trust and to love Jesus as their Savior. —R. W. D.

GODLY MOTHERS NOT ONLY BRING YOU UP, THEY BRING YOU TO GOD.

He counts the number of the stars; He calls them all by name.

PSALM 147:4

Astronomers used Australia's largest optical telescope to map 100,000 galaxies that surround our own galaxy, the Milky Way. The 3-dimensional map covers 5 percent of the sky and allows us to see 4 billion light-years deep into space. The number of stars included defies our imagination, but not the knowledge of God.

How amazing to read, "He counts the number of the stars; He calls them all by name." Jesus Christ, the creator of the galaxies, visited our planet to pay the penalty for our sin and open the way to friendship and fellowship with Him. Today He stands ready to bring healing and wholeness to our deeply wounded spirits. From naming stars to mending hearts, nothing is too hard for God. —D. C. M.

IN CREATION WE SEE GOD'S HAND;
IN REDEMPTION WE SEE HIS HEART.

God demonstrates His own love toward us, in that
while we were still sinners, Christ died for us.

ROMANS 5:8

From the cradle to the grave, we all need love. How vividly this is illustrated in the song "Jesus Loves Me" by Anna B. Warner (1824–1915). She and her sister Susan were gifted novelists. Anna also published many poems. The familiar lines of "Jesus Loves Me" were penned in 1860 as a poem of comfort spoken to a dying child in one of Susan's stories. Today it's sung by children and adults around the world.

When a famous theologian visited a leading US seminary, a student asked him, "What is the greatest single thought that ever crossed your mind?" Expecting a profound theological answer, the class waited breathlessly for his reply. He bowed his head in thought and then slowly lifted his head and said, "Jesus loves me, this I know, for the Bible tells me so." —D. J. D.

THE CROSS OF JESUS IS THE SUPREME
EVIDENCE OF THE LOVE OF GOD.

He shall stand and feed His flock . . . in the
majesty of the name of the LORD His God.

MICAH 5:4

Can meekness and majesty exist in the same person? Amazingly, they co-existed in the God-man, Jesus.

He was humble and meek. He didn't insist on luxury or seek for material possessions. In fact, He didn't own or possess any property except for the clothes He wore. In terms of pursuing fame and glory, He walked away from more crowds than He called together. He was the leader, but He knelt to wash the feet of His disciples (John 13).

Yet, with such beautiful humility, there was also an awesome majesty about Jesus. One word or look from Jesus could quiet a crowd, calm a storm, or make a disciple weep. Thousands followed Him as He lived and taught with unequaled power and authority. Although He died bearing our sin and shame, He rose from the grave in glory. One day He will return in majesty as King of kings and Lord of lords, vanquishing His foes and judging the nations. —D. C. E.

THE HIGH AND HOLY ONE BECAME THE MEEK AND LOWLY ONE.

You, O LORD, are a shield for me,
my glory and the One who lifts up my head.

PSALM 3:3

In 1992 the Summer Olympic Games were held in Barcelona, Spain. One of the runners in the 400-meter race was an English athlete named Derek Redmond. He had trained for years to compete in the Olympics. But while sprinting in a qualifying heat, he suddenly pulled a hamstring and crumpled to the track in pain.

Determined to go on, Derek struggled to his feet. He was hobbling toward the finish line when his father scaled the retaining wall and jumped onto the track. Before anyone could stop him, Jim Redmond reached his son. The young runner leaned on his father's shoulder as he staggered to complete the race. The entire crowd stood and cheered the two men on. When they crossed the finish line, it was as if the runner, his father, and the spectators had done it together.

It takes all of our spiritual stamina to complete the course of life, but we don't run the course alone. Christ Himself runs with us.
—H. W. R.

WE ARE JUDGED BY HOW WE FINISH, NOT BY HOW WE START.

Do not be like the horse or like the mule, . . .
which must be harnessed with bit and bridle.

PSALM 32:9

This is a brand-new horse," my sister-in-law said as she stood next to the mare who had bucked her off several weeks before. She told me that after a skilled trainer had spent time with the horse, the animal had returned with a new personality.

She explained, "Before, this horse's attitude was, 'Go away; don't bother me.' Now, when I approach her, it's as if she's saying, 'What would you like me to do?' I don't know how the trainer did it, but my horse has a whole new outlook on life."

The conversation caused me to think of God's command in Psalm 32:9. He said, "Do not be like the horse or like the mule, which have no understanding, which must be harnessed with bit and bridle, else they will not come near you." The psalm speaks of knowing God in a relationship characterized by guidance, trust, and joy.

When we are yielded to God, we welcome His approach. There is no need for the spiritual bit and bridle when we serve Him from the heart. —D. C. M.

OBEDIENCE FROM THE HEART IS WANTING
TO DO WHAT GOD TELLS YOU TO DO.

*Philip opened his mouth, and beginning
at this Scripture, preached Jesus to him.*

ACTS 8:35

Shortly after the novel *Gone With The Wind* had been published, a young woman sat beside a history professor at a dinner. Trying to make conversation, she asked him if he had read it. "No," the professor answered. The woman admonished, "You'd better hurry up. It's been out 6 weeks." Then the professor inquired, "Have you read Dante's *Divine Comedy*?" "No," the woman said. The professor responded, "You'd better hurry up. It's been out 600 years."

These days, new books dealing with all sorts of subjects pour from printing presses in an overwhelming cascade. Even if we did nothing but read all day every day, we couldn't keep up with the output. So we must discriminate and decide what we'll read and what we'll ignore.

Important as many books are, only the Bible reveals the good news about Jesus (Acts 8:35). Only the Bible teaches us how to please Him. So let's make sure we give the Bible the priority it deserves. It's a "must read." —V. C. G.

MANY BOOKS CAN INFORM, BUT ONLY THE BIBLE CAN TRANSFORM.

*He first found his own brother Simon,
and said to him, "We have found the Messiah."*

JOHN 1:41

Years ago some prospectors were panning for gold in Montana when one of them found an unusual stone. Breaking it open, he saw that it contained gold. Working eagerly, the men soon discovered an abundance of the precious metal. With unrestrained delight they shouted, "We've found it! We've found gold! We're rich!"

Before going into town for supplies, they agreed not to tell a soul about their find. While in town, not one of them breathed a word about their discovery. When they were about to return to camp, though, a group of men had gathered and were ready to follow them.

"You've found gold," the group said. "Who told you?" asked the prospectors. "No one," they replied. "Your faces showed it!"

It's much like that when a person discovers Christ. The joy of sins forgiven and a new relationship with Him shows in a transformed life. Finding Christ is life's greatest discovery, and this is good news we don't want to keep a secret! —R. W. D.

THE GOOD NEWS OF CHRIST IS TOO GOOD TO KEEP TO YOURSELF.

Her children rise up and call her blessed; her husband also.

PROVERBS 31:28

What is a mother's idea of a dream home? A one-story, ranch-style house on a half-acre lot with a fenced-in yard for the children? Three bedrooms, two large bathrooms, a big family room, a modern kitchen, and a two-car garage? Or maybe her dream home would have a beautiful garden and a view overlooking a quiet lake.

As good as these features may be, most mothers know it takes more to make a house a home. The most important characteristics of a home are the spiritual qualities and the love between father, mother, and children.

A loving, spiritual atmosphere is the feature most desired in a home, and that can be found in a simple one-room house or in a spacious mansion. I think we would all agree that love for our family and the fear of the Lord can turn any house into a dream home. It's a place where Mom—and the rest of the family—will find true joy.
—M. R. D. II

A HOUSE IS BUILT BY HUMAN HANDS, A HOME BY HUMAN HEARTS.

Do business till I come.

LUKE 19:13

In the days before Connecticut became a state, the colonial legislature was in session when a thick darkness blotted out the sunlight. The cry was heard, "It is the day of judgment! Let us go home and get ready!"

But one member of the legislature, an old church deacon, stood up and said, "Brethren, it may be the day of judgment—I do not know. The Lord may come. But when He does, I want Him to find me at my post, doing my duty. Mr. Speaker, I move that candles be brought in and we get on with the business of the colony."

In Luke 19:11–27, Jesus told a parable of a nobleman who went into a far country. Before leaving, the man called 10 of his servants together, gave them each a coin worth about 3 months' salary, and said, "Do business till I come." Later he returned, and the servants had to give an account of what they had done with the money.

At His ascension, Jesus also "went into a far country" (Luke 19:12), and He could return at any moment. But until He does, our duty as His servants is to serve Him. —R. W. D.

A WATCHING CHRISTIAN WILL BE A WORKING CHRISTIAN.

He brought me up out of a horrible pit.

PSALM 40:2

The psalmist said that God "put a new song" in his mouth (Ps. 40:3). The song did not come easily to him though. "He . . . brought me up out of a horrible pit" (v. 2).

A Chinese scholar who converted to Christ told this parable: "A man fell into a dark, dirty pit, and he tried to climb out but he couldn't. Confucius came along. He saw the man in the pit and said, 'Poor fellow. If he had listened to me, he never would have fallen in.' And he left. Buddha came along and saw the man in the pit and said, 'Poor fellow. If he can climb up here, I'll help him.' And he too left. Then Christ came and said, 'Poor fellow!' And He jumped into the pit and helped him out."

God rescued the psalmist from the "pit." And He gave him a new song to sing, which we too can sing if we've experienced God's deliverance from trouble. —H. W. R.

**GOD'S DAWN OF DELIVERANCE OFTEN COMES
WHEN THE HOUR OF TRIAL IS DARKEST.**

Forever, O LORD, Your Word is settled in heaven.

PSALM 119:89

Someone has written a poem that talks about the problem of using a spell-checking program on a computer. The first stanza says:

I have a spelling checker

I disk covered four my PC.

It plane lee marks four my revue

Miss steaks aye can knot see.

It's proof positive that if you're looking to the wrong source for correctness, then you aren't right.

It's like that with matters of faith. It is possible to trust the wrong source of information about spiritual things. Where can we go for the truth? We need a perfect, fool-proof source. That source is the Bible. God's Word is the only source of what is true and right. —J. D. B.

LIKE A COMPASS, THE BIBLE ALWAYS POINTS YOU IN THE RIGHT DIRECTION.

Your hands have made me and fashioned me.

PSALM 119:73

Have you ever noticed the pock-marks, or dimples, covering the surface of a golf ball? They make the ball look imperfect. So what's their purpose?

An aeronautical engineer who designs golf balls says that a perfectly smooth ball would travel only about 130 yards off the tee. But the same ball with the right kind of dimples will fly twice that far. These apparent "flaws" minimize the ball's air resistance and allow it to travel much farther.

Most of us can quickly name the physical characteristics we wish we had been born without. It's difficult to imagine that these "imperfections" are there for a purpose and are part of God's master design. The "dimples" we dislike may enable us to bring the greatest glory to our wise and loving Creator, who knows how to get the best out of us. —D. C. M.

EVERY CHILD OF GOD HAS A SPECIAL PLACE IN HIS PLAN.

When Christ . . . appears, then you also will appear with Him in glory.

COLOSSIANS 3:4

By the end of his life, musician Giuseppe Verdi was recognized as a master of dramatic composition. But he didn't begin his career with such success. As a youth, he had obvious musical ability, but he was denied entrance to the Milan Conservatory because he lacked the required education and background.

Yet time does strange things. After Verdi's fame had spread worldwide, the school was renamed the Verdi Conservatory of Music.

Verdi's experience reminds me of the experience of our Lord and of all who trust in Him. The Son of God was rejected by His countrymen because they didn't feel He had adequate training or the right family background (Matt. 13:53–58). Even though Jesus spoke the truth and His works spoke for themselves, He did not receive the recognition He deserved. Yet someday everyone will bow before Him and give Him the honor due His name (Phil. 2:9–11). —M. R. D. II

ALL THAT WE LONG TO BECOME WILL
FIND FULFILLMENT WHEN WE SEE JESUS.

He has borne our griefs and carried our sorrows.

ISAIAH 53:4

The Vietnam Veterans Memorial was dedicated in 1982. In the first 15 years, 54,000 items were left at the Wall. It still takes almost an hour every night, and much longer on Memorial Day, to collect the mementos—a teddy bear, a photo of a soldier's grandchild, a letter from a daughter who never knew her dad.

Every item is labeled and taken to a warehouse. No one knows quite how to deal with it all. "No one ever expected this to happen," a park ranger says. "It's so personal. It caught everyone by surprise."

Loss comes to us all, and we often carry our grief for many years. We struggle with our emotions. Is there a place where we can leave our sorrows and find healing for the wounds of life? We can bring our grief to the Man of sorrows. There is help and healing and closure at the cross for the deepest pain of our hearts. —D. C. M.

LEAVE YOUR SORROWS WITH THE "MAN OF SORROWS."

*You shall receive power when the Holy Spirit has
come upon you; and you shall be witnesses to Me.*

ACTS 1:8

John, do you want to spend the rest of your life selling
sugared water, or do you want a chance to change the world?"
That was the challenge Steve Jobs issued in 1983 to John
Sculley, then president of Pepsi-Cola. Mr. Jobs was the creative genius
behind Apple Computer. He knew that the soft-drink executive could
help Apple make its mark on the computer world. Sculley accepted
the bold challenge.

Jesus issued a challenge to three fishermen as they tended their
nets. He commanded, "Follow Me!" (Mark. 1:17). They did, and with
a handful of other ordinary men they changed the world.

We can either follow the world's dead-end philosophies, or we
can accept Jesus' challenge to bring change to the world. —V. C. G.

**A DISCIPLE IS KNOWN NOT FOR WHAT HE
GIVES UP, BUT FOR WHAT HE TAKES UP.**

Put on tender mercies, kindness, humility, meekness, longsuffering.

COLOSSIANS 3:12

In 1975, John Molloy wrote a book called *Dress for Success,* which became the fashion guidebook for many people trying to climb the corporate ladder. Molloy's advice centered on a basic premise—always dress like your boss.

Every day, for work, school, or recreation, we all have to decide what to wear. And even in a dress-down society people strive for the right look. But we must also make choices about another wardrobe— our attitudes and actions. If we claim to be followers of Christ, our spiritual apparel is of far greater significance than our physical clothing.

Take a look at God's dress code for us. As His chosen people, we are to clothe ourselves with "kindness, humility, meekness, longsuffering" (Col. 3:12). We are to demonstrate patience and forgiveness (v. 13). And above all, we must "put on love, which is the bond of perfection" (v. 14). —D. C. M.

KINDNESS IS CHRISTIANITY WITH ITS WORKING CLOTHES ON.

Jesus Christ is the same yesterday, today, and forever.

HEBREWS 13:8

Bill Irwin, a friend of mine who is blind, has a talking computer he uses to study the Bible. He's had a few chuckles over some of the pronunciations. "For a long time," Bill says, "the computer pronounced Holy Bible as 'holly bibble' until I figured out how to modify it."

But there was one thing Bill couldn't change. The computer uses the Spanish pronunciation for Jesus Christ—HEYsus Krist. "The programmer is Hispanic," Bill told me with a smile, "and he made sure that HEYsus Krist cannot be altered."

I like that. It reminds me that among the things in life that can be changed to suit my taste, one remains tamper-resistant—I can't change Jesus. When life is unsettled, I gain great comfort from the Bible's affirmation that "Jesus Christ is the same yesterday, today, and forever." —D. C. M.

**IN A WORLD OF CONSTANT CHANGE,
YOU CAN TRUST THE UNCHANGING CHRIST.**

Forever, O LORD, Your Word is settled in heaven.

PSALM 119:89

*L*ouisa May Alcott's *Little Women* and Jane Austen's *Sense and Sensibility* became popular again when film producers put their stories on the screen. But hasn't our society advanced so far that yesteryear's books couldn't possibly have any relevance to today's situations?

The great thing about classic literature is that just the opposite is true. Fine writing has enduring value when it speaks to the heart-issues people have always shared—issues like relationships, love, and surviving in this world.

But there's one old book that tops them all. It stands above the rest not only because it speaks clearly and accurately about the human condition but also because it was inspired by the One who created us. It's the Bible, God's Word to us. When it talks about marriage, it's right on target. When it talks about how to treat others, it's more helpful than today's advice column. But most important, when it talks about the purpose of life, it's the only source of truth. —J. D. B.

**TO STAY ON COURSE, TRUST THE
UNFAILING COMPASS OF GOD'S WORD.**

When He had sent them away,
He departed to the mountain to pray.

MARK 6:46

When a whitewater raft guide shouts, "Eddy out!" he doesn't mean, "Throw someone named Edward out of the boat!" It's the command for the people on one side to hold their paddles against the current while the others stroke. This turns the raft out of the swift water and into the quiet eddies along the river's edge.

Shooting the rapids is exciting but tiring. When the guide sees that everyone needs a break, he says, "Eddy out!"

During Jesus' last 3 years on earth, the velocity of His life increased dramatically. He was teaching, healing, and constantly being mobbed by needy people. There was enough work to keep Christ busy 24 hours a day. Yet, in the Gospels we see Jesus' pattern: "When He had sent them away, He departed to the mountain to pray."

Perhaps your opportunities and achievements are coming hard and fast lately. Now is the most important word in your vocabulary. But along the river of life, there's a time to paddle and a time to "Eddy out!" Make sure you're listening to your Guide. —D. C. M.

TO AVOID A BREAKDOWN, TAKE A BREAK FOR REST AND PRAYER.

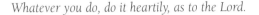

Whatever you do, do it heartily, as to the Lord.

COLOSSIANS 3:23

On the 80th birthday of the famous musician and conductor Arturo Toscanini, someone asked his son what he considered to be his father's greatest achievement. He replied, "For him there can be no such thing. Whatever he happens to be doing at any moment is the biggest undertaking in his life, whether it be conducting a symphony or peeling an orange."

Toscanini gave himself so completely to every task that he could become totally involved in peeling an orange or in conducting a symphony. How much more we as God's children should take continual delight in the deeds of love we do for the Lord and for others!

Whether we are engaged in a project of great magnitude or simply helping a neighbor, we must consider our responsibility to God and man. The apostle Paul said, "Anything we do for Jesus, whether large or small, should be 'the biggest thing' in our lives." —R. W. D.

IT'S A GREAT THING TO DO A LITTLE THING WELL.

*He who believes in Me, . . . out of his
heart will flow rivers of living water.*

JOHN 7:38

The Dead Sea is so salty that it contains no fish or plant life. What accounts for this unusual condition? There are absolutely no outlets! A great volume of water pours into this area, but nothing flows out. Many inlets plus no outlets equals a dead sea.

This law of nature may also be applied to the child of God, and it explains why many believers are so unfruitful and lacking in spiritual vitality. It's possible for some people to attend Bible conferences, listen to religious broadcasts, study the Scriptures, and continually take in the Word as it is preached from the pulpit, and yet seem lifeless and unproductive in their Christian lives. Such individuals are like the Dead Sea. They have several "inlets" but no "outlets." To be vibrant and useful believers, we must not only "take in" all we can, but we must also "give out" in service to others!

May the Lord make us refreshing fountains where thirsty souls may drink. —R. W. D.

**TO BE A CHANNEL OF BLESSING,
LET CHRIST'S LOVE FLOW THROUGH YOU.**

Do not provoke your children to wrath,
but bring them up in the training . . . of the Lord.

EPHESIANS 6:4

Benjamin West was just trying to be a good babysitter for his little sister Sally. While his mother was out, he found some bottles of colored ink and proceeded to paint Sally's portrait. But by the time Mrs. West returned, ink blots stained the table, chairs, and floor. Benjamin's mother surveyed the mess without a word until she saw the picture. Picking it up she exclaimed, "Why, it's Sally!" And she bent down and kissed her young son.

In 1763, when he was 25 years old, Benjamin West was selected as history painter to England's King George III. He became one of the most celebrated artists of his day. Commenting on his start as an artist, he said, "My mother's kiss made me a painter."

What a challenge to raise our children according to God's standards, knowing when to say, "It's a mess!" and when to say, "Why, it's Sally!" —D. C. M.

CORRECTION DOES MUCH; ENCOURAGEMENT DOES MORE.

*Do not be conformed to this world, but be
transformed by the renewing of your mind.*

ROMANS 12:2

First, the bad news. Our society can have a terrible influence on us and our children. The entertainment media, for example, offer various forms of sinful behavior for our listening and viewing "pleasure." One music TV channel, for instance, was characterized in *World* magazine by film critic Michael Medved like this: "There is absolutely no excuse for MTV to be present in the home. It is 100-percent negative."

And now for the good news. None of society's negative influences have to bother you. They will affect you and your family only if you let them. They can infiltrate the minds of you and your children only if you refuse to use the discernment, power, and instruction God has provided to everyone who is redeemed by faith in His Son Jesus Christ (Eph. 4:20–24). We should find great comfort in knowing that the Lord has given us the resources to live above society's degradation, His Spirit and His Word. —J. D. B.

**YIELD TO THE SPIRIT, AND YOU WON'T
BE CONFORMED TO THE WORLD.**

Another book was opened, which is the Book of Life.

REVELATION 20:12

Late one afternoon in 19th-century London, two sight-seeing soldiers went to visit the magnificent Westminster Abbey but found its doors locked. Arthur Stanley, who had become dean of the Abbey in 1863, was walking outside at the time and noticed them. When he learned that they couldn't return the next day, he unlocked the door and gave them a personal tour.

As they walked through that awe-inspiring building, Stanley talked about the honor of being immortalized by having one's name inscribed on a monument inside. Then he added, "You may have a more enduring monument than this, for this building will molder into dust and be forgotten, but you, if your names are written in the Lamb's Book of Life, will abide forever." Before parting, he urged them to receive Christ as their Savior. "If we never meet on earth again," he said, "we will certainly meet in heaven." That day they made sure of their salvation.

Are you sure that your name appears in the Lamb's Book of Life? —V. C. G.

YOUR NAME IS WRITTEN IN HEAVEN BY TRUSTING CHRIST ON EARTH.

The integrity of the upright will guide them.

PROVERBS 11:3

I'll always remember the day when as a child I found two coins on the school playground. I brought them home, thinking they wouldn't be missed. But Mother made me take them to my teacher. "They belong to someone else," Mother told me. Since then, God has often reminded me of this early lesson in honesty.

For example, recently as I was putting bags of groceries in my car, I discovered at the bottom of the cart a greeting card I hadn't paid for. I marched back to the cash register, waited in line, apologized for the oversight, and paid for the card. A man behind me, looking dumbfounded, challenged me, "It's only a greeting card! Who would have known? Weren't you a bit silly to come back?"

For a split second I did feel silly. But then these words came to mind: "Should you ever lose your wallet," I replied smiling, "I'm sure you hope that somebody silly like me finds it!" —J. E. Y.

HONESTY'S REWARD IS SOMETHING MONEY CANNOT BUY—A CLEAR CONSCIENCE BEFORE GOD.

Your Word is very pure; therefore Your servant loves it.

PSALM 119:140

In an excavation at Jerusalem, archaeologist Gabriel Barkay uncovered a small copper scroll with writing on it from the Bible. This fragment of Scripture was brittle and tarnished with age. Barkay took it to his laboratory and worked with unbelievable patience and delicate care to unroll it without destroying it.

Dated around 400 B.C., the scroll was a very important find because it contained the earliest written Hebrew name for God, Yahweh (or Jehovah). Apparently the scribe who copied it had broken with the practice of never writing that sacred name. Always before, because of their reverence for its holiness, Jewish scribes had felt unworthy to pen that special name.

The Bible is God's holy, infallible Word, and we must handle its truths with the same care Barkay gave to his discovery and the same reverence the copyists gave to God's name. Scripture comes to us from God's heart. We must guard its message with integrity and handle it with care. —D. C. E.

READ YOUR BIBLE PRAYERFULLY AND OBEY IT JOYFULLY.

Whatever a man sows, that he will also reap.

GALATIANS 6:7

A woman gave her teenage son a used automobile. The youth enjoyed racing the car around curves so he could hear the tires squeal. One morning his car skidded and smashed into a telephone pole. The boy was thrown through the windshield and rushed to a hospital. When his pastor reached the hospital, the boy's mother was frantic. She grasped the pastor's hands in hers and exclaimed, "Why would God let this happen?"

Her question is understandable, but it misses the hard truth of the situation. She can't blame God for that accident. If the Lord were to suspend the laws of physics and snatch a telephone pole from in front of her son, He might just as well place one in front of someone else who was driving carefully.

God doesn't cancel the rule of sowing and reaping just because we become Christians. But there is an upside to that principle. If we sow "to the Spirit [we] will of the Spirit reap everlasting life" (Gal. 6:8). —H. W. R.

THE LAW OF SOWING AND REAPING HAS NEVER BEEN REPEALED.

Search me, O God, and know my heart.

PSALM 139:23

The Learning Annex, a chain of adult-education schools, says that more than 200,000 people have completed its popular class on controlling household clutter. Who takes the course? People who keep empty mayonnaise jars, manuals for appliances they no longer have, broken buttons, out-of-date phone books, and keys to houses they lived in 20 years ago.

Household clutter occupies space, saps energy, and creates frustration. Spiritual clutter is much the same—unresolved conflicts pile up in our hearts; unconfessed sins gather a thick layer of guilt; unspoken prayers litter our minds.

How can we clean out our jumbled lives? God's Word tells us how.

➤ Unresolved conflicts: "If your brother sins against you, go and tell him his fault" (Matt. 18:15).

➤ Unconfessed sin: "If we confess our sins, He is faithful and just to forgive us our sins" (1 John 1:9).

—D. C. M.

TO GET YOUR LIFE IN ORDER, PUT GOD FIRST.

In You, O LORD, I put my trust.

PSALM 31:1

In an article for *Campus Life* magazine, Susan Smart describes her third—and nearly last—solo flight. She had been practicing a maneuver at 5,000 feet when she lost control and her Cessna 150 began spinning wildly toward earth. After several seconds of panic, she recalled her instructor's words: "If you ever go into a spin in a Cessna 150, just let go of the controls. It's built to fly on its own."

Susan shouted to herself several times, "Let go!" Finally, she yanked her hands from the controls and covered her face. After some wild yawing and pitching, the plane returned to level flight. She had fallen more than half a mile, but she survived because she had the faith to let go.

Her experience vividly illustrates what it means to trust God in a time of crisis. In Psalm 31, David cried out to the Lord in his time of trouble. He knew that his only hope was to put his situation in God's hands and rely on Him.

Is your life in a spin? Let go of the controls! —D. C. E.

THE BEST WAY TO HANDLE A PROBLEM IS TO HAND IT OVER TO GOD.

Ask for the old paths, where the good way is, and walk in it.

JEREMIAH 6:16

I seldom yearn for "the good old days." The quality of today's cars, for example, far exceeds that of my first one, a 1935 model with only a manifold heater and a short lifespan. When somebody says, "They don't make them like they used to," I reply, "I'm sure glad they don't."

I do long, however, for a return to the "old paths, where the good way is" (Jer. 6:16). There was a time when schoolchildren were taught kindness, purity, loyalty, obedience to authority, and reverence for God. Back then, newspaper and magazine articles reflected the belief that we are moral beings who should exercise self-restraint and seek the good of others.

Today, this idea has largely been scrapped and replaced with the concept that we can be happy only when we have freedom to fulfill our every selfish desire. We need not be discouraged, however. God is still in control. We can show the way by loving people and praying for them.

—H. V. L.

**OUR PURPOSE ON EARTH IS NOT TO GET USED
TO THE DARK BUT TO WALK IN THE LIGHT.**

They cried out to the LORD in their trouble,
and He saved them out of their distresses.

PSALM 107:19

A farmer and his son were working together out in the field. The father told the boy to throw all the large stones he could find into a nearby ditch so they would not interfere with plowing. After working a long time, the son called out, "Dad, there's one rock here I can't move even though I've tried my hardest."

"No, son," replied the father, "you haven't tried your hardest until you've called out to me for help. I can give you the strength you need."

The father then came alongside the boy and added his strength. Together, they moved the stubborn rock with ease.

Too often we try our hardest to carry some heavy burden or work out a difficult problem, but with no success. After having done our best, we wonder why we have met with nothing but failure. Lovingly and patiently our heavenly Father reminds us that we must learn to depend on Him, and that we haven't tried our hardest until we've called on Him for help. —H. G. B.

GOD'S ABILITY IS NOT LIMITED BY OUR INABILITY.

Aquila and Priscilla . . . explained to [Apollos] the way of God.

ACTS 18:26

Where can we find a marriage that works? How about the story of a couple who not only made their marriage work but who also used their unity to assist the early church? Their names were Aquila and Priscilla. Notice the characteristics that made them helpful to Paul, and which, I believe, reflected the strength of their marriage.

They were selfless and brave. In Romans 16:4, Paul said they "risked their own necks" for him.

They were hospitable. A church met in their home (1 Cor. 16:19).

They were flexible. Twice they had to move—once by force from Rome (Acts 18:2) and once by choice to go on a missions trip with Paul (v. 18).

They worked together. They were tentmakers (v. 3).

They both were committed to Christ and teaching others about Him. Aquila and Priscilla were a team. —J. D. B.

MARRIAGE WORKS BEST WHEN A COUPLE HAS A SINGLE PURPOSE.

I have chosen the way of truth.

PSALM 119:30

A story is told of a man who loved old books. He met an acquaintance who had just thrown away a Bible that had been stored in the attic of his ancestral home for generations. "I couldn't read it," the friend explained. "Somebody named Gutensomething had printed it." "Not Gutenberg!" the book lover exclaimed in horror. "That Bible was one of the first books ever printed. Why, a copy just sold for over two million dollars!"

His friend was unimpressed. "Mine wouldn't have brought a dollar. Some fellow named Martin Luther had scribbled all over it in German."

This man treated as worthless that which was valuable. We had better be careful of the "bargains" we make in life. Our culture places a high price tag on what is worthless and throws away as worthless what is of eternal value. Ask the Lord to help you discern what's worth keeping and what is best discarded. —H. W. R.

THE CHOICES WE MAKE CHART THE COURSE OF LIFE WE TAKE.

We will [tell] to the generation to come the praises of the LORD.

PSALM 78:4

Imagine an evening in ancient Israel. The day's work is done, the meal is finished, and the family is gathered around a small fire that pushes away the night chill and casts a soft glow on their faces. It's story time.

Father and grandfather take turns relating to the children the "praises of the LORD" (Ps. 78:4). They tell of Abraham's journey. They speak of Isaac. Their voices come alive when they tell about old Jacob. They remember Moses and Joshua and Elijah and the great King David. They recount the history of their own family. And all the time they focus their attention on the mighty works of God in behalf of His people.

Our children need to know about God. They need to learn from us about His love, His faithfulness, and His grace. They need to hear from us about the times He stepped into our lives to protect and provide. Tell your sons and daughters and grandchildren how God has worked in your life. —D. C. E.

A GODLY PARENT IS A CHILD'S BEST GUIDE TO GOD.

Pleasant words are like a honeycomb, sweetness to the soul.

PROVERBS 16:24

In Ohio stands a courthouse that has an unusual location. Raindrops that fall on the north side of the building go into Lake Ontario and the Gulf of St. Lawrence, while those falling on the south side go into the Mississippi River and the Gulf of Mexico. At precisely the point of the peak of the roof, just a gentle puff of wind can determine the destiny of many raindrops. It will make a difference of more than 2,000 miles as to their final destination.

The spiritual application is clear. By the smallest deed or choice of words we might set in motion influences that could change the course of others' lives here and now, and could also affect their eternal destiny. An unkind word or a thoughtless act can do much damage. On the other hand, a kind word, a helpful deed, a pat on the back, a sincere testimony for Christ may accomplish much good. Any one of these little things could encourage, give renewed hope, and even be used of God to bring a person to Christ. —R. W. D.

LIFE'S BIG TURNING POINTS OFTEN HINGE ON LITTLE THINGS.

What manner of love the Father has bestowed on us,
that we should be called children of God!

1 JOHN 3:1

Where do kids get the stuff they come up with? One evening as I was getting 8-year-old Steven settled in for the night, he looked at me and said, "You're my second favorite dad." Whoa, I thought. Am I missing something here? But then Steve quickly filled me in. "First, God. He's my number one Father. Then you."

I'm glad Steven is able to transfer his feelings of love for his earthly father to his heavenly Father. But some people have a tough time accepting that "other Father." All they know of a father on earth is desertion, abuse, neglect, hatred, and pain. To those who have seen nothing but bad from an earthly dad, turning their life over to another Father—even one who is God—is not easy. But it is not impossible.

If you struggle with loving the One who is our heavenly Father, remember that He is the ultimate Dad because He epitomizes love, grace, mercy, and compassion. —J. D. B.

A GOOD FATHER REFLECTS THE LOVE OF THE HEAVENLY FATHER.

Have you not even read this Scripture?

MARK 12:10

*B*ooks! Books! Books! Hardcovers and paperbacks. Reference works and joke books. Romantic novels and mysteries. Self-help books and religious publications. They just keep appearing—and we keep buying them.

We also keep writing them. No wonder Solomon said, "Of making many books there is no end" (Eccl. 12:12).

Jill Briscoe was addressing a convention of religious writers and editors. An author of several books and numerous articles, she was talking about what it means to have people read your words and be influenced by your writing. She called it a privilege and a responsibility.

Then Mrs. Briscoe made this provocative statement: "When we get to heaven," she said, "we will not say to God, 'Did You read my book?' Rather, God will say to us, 'Did you read My Book?'" —D. C. E.

**THERE'S A BIG DIFFERENCE BETWEEN THE BOOKS
MEN MAKE AND THE BOOK THAT MAKES MEN.**

He is a rewarder of those who diligently seek Him.

HEBREWS 11:6

An atheist said to a Quaker, "Have you ever seen God? Have you ever felt God? Have you ever smelled God? And you say you have a God!"

After a long pause, the Quaker replied, "Hast thou ever seen thy brains? Hast thou ever felt thy brains? Hast thou ever smelled thy brains? And thou sayest thou hast brains!"

There probably are very few atheists—those who have seriously thought about life and concluded that there is no God. There are more agnostics—thinking people who say, "I don't know." The vast majority of individuals, however, affirm—at least intellectually—that God exists.

Hebrews 11:6 tells us that recognizing God's existence is the first step to knowing Him personally. Then we must seek Him and believe that He will reward our quest to know Him. —D. J. D.

GOD REVEALS HE IS THERE BY HIS MERCY, LOVE, AND CARE.

Your rod and Your staff, they comfort me.

PSALM 23:4

*A*uthor H. W. McLaughlin tells of visiting Israel and talking to an old shepherd. Thinking about Psalm 23, McLaughlin asked him how he used his staff to comfort and guide the sheep.

The elderly man said that in the daylight he always carried it across his shoulders so the sheep could see it. Somehow this reassured them of his presence and protection. He further explained that if darkness overtook him before he had brought the sheep to a safe resting place for the night, or if they were caught in a heavy fog, he would walk slowly while tapping it on the ground. Although the sheep could not see the staff, they could hear the tapping and would follow the sound, knowing their shepherd was just ahead.

God's inspired Word is to the Christian what that staff was to those sheep, reassuring us of God's presence, protection, and provision by day and by night. Sometimes we see His leading from Scripture very clearly. At other times we must listen with special care to His Spirit.
—H. G. B.

YOU CAN TRUST WHERE YOU ARE GOING WHEN GOD IS LEADING.

Casting all your care upon Him, for He cares for you.

1 PETER 5:7

Isaac Page tells the story of a poor man in Ireland who was plodding along toward home, carrying a huge sack of potatoes. A horse and wagon came along and the driver stopped to offer him a ride. The man accepted and climbed up on the seat alongside the driver but kept holding the bag of potatoes in his arms. When the driver suggested that he lay it down on the wagon floor, he replied warmly in his Irish brogue, "I don't like to trouble you too much, sir. You're a givin' me a ride already, so I'll just carry the potatoes!"

We do the same when we try to carry life's burdens by worrying instead of turning them over to God. No wonder we become weary, our hearts faint within us, and we lose courage. Any circumstance over which we have no control can become a "bag of potatoes" if we fret and worry about the outcome. So the next time you start worrying, let God carry the burden for you. —H. G. B.

GOD WANTS US TO BURDEN HIM WITH WHATEVER BURDENS US.

This thing is too much for you;
you are not able to perform it by yourself.

EXODUS 18:18

In a horse-pulling contest at a county fair the first-place horse moved a sled weighing 4,500 pounds. The runner-up pulled 4,000 pounds. The owners of the two horses wondered how much the animals could pull if they worked together. So they hitched them up and loaded the sled. To everyone's surprise, the horses were able to pull 12,000 pounds.

Sometimes in the Lord's work we try to pull the weight of a job all by ourselves. However, when we team up with others we work with greater efficiency and can accomplish so much more.

That's what happened with Moses when the Israelites came to him to settle their disputes. At first he worked alone. His judgments were effective, but his method was inefficient. His father-in-law, who saw that he would soon wear down, advised him to handle only the difficult cases and let other wise leaders take the easier ones. Moses heeded his advice. He increased his efficiency, and much more work was accomplished. —J. D. B.

TEAMWORK DIVIDES THE EFFORT AND MULTIPLIES THE EFFECT.

Judge not, and you shall not be judged.

LUKE 6:37

A man was having difficulty communicating with his wife and concluded that she was becoming hard of hearing. So he decided to conduct a test without her knowing about it.

One evening he sat in a chair on the far side of the room. Her back was to him and she could not see him. Very quietly he whispered, "Can you hear me?" There was no response.

Moving a little closer, he asked again, "Can you hear me now?" Still no reply. Quietly he edged closer and whispered the same words, but still no answer. Finally, he moved right in behind her chair and said, "Can you hear me now?" To his surprise and chagrin she responded with irritation in her voice, "For the *fourth* time, yes!"

What a warning to us about judging! Jesus knew human nature well. That's why He said, "Judge not, and you shall not be judged." —R. W. D.

IF YOU ARE LOOKING FOR FAULTS TO CORRECT, TRY LOOKING IN A MIRROR.

He who is slow to anger allays contention.

PROVERBS 15:18

Anger is a strong, potentially destructive emotion. When you are personally offended and your feelings are hurt, for example, it's always best to check that immediate reaction of wanting to "tell someone off." Confrontation to resolve a difference may be necessary, but using restraint, allowing time to cool off, is always wise.

The story is told of a young man who had been insulted by an acquaintance and was very indignant. "I'm going at once to demand an apology," he insisted. "My dear boy," cautioned a wise, old man, "take a word of advice from one who loves peace. An insult is like mud; it will brush off much better when it dries. Wait till you and he are both cool, and the thing will be easily solved. If you go now, it will only be to quarrel." The young man heeded that counsel, and the next day the person who had insulted him came to ask for his forgiveness.

The next time you get angry count slowly to 100 and remember that time and God are on your side. —D. J. D .

ANGER IS JUST ONE LETTER SHORT OF DANGER.

O LORD, how manifold are Your works!
In wisdom You have made them all.

PSALM 104:24

A tiny bird, the lesser white-throat warbler, summers in Germany and winters in Africa. As the days grow short, the adult birds head south, leaving their little ones behind. Several weeks later, the young fly across thousands of miles of unfamiliar land and sea to join their parents. How do they find a place totally unknown to them? Experiments have shown that they have an instinctive knowledge of longitude, latitude, and an ability to tell direction by the stars. God has given them a calendar, a clock, and all the navigational data they need to fly those thousands of uncharted miles to their parents' side.

The evolutionist says that our amazing and complex world developed by chance. But is this easier to accept than to believe that God created this amazing warbler, and thousands of other such creatures? To me, ascribing this to chance is absurd.

God's wisdom is plainly observable in the works of His creation. His handiwork in nature speaks for His existence and power. —D. C. E.

**HE IS SPIRITUALLY DEAF WHO CANNOT
HEAR THE VOICE OF GOD IN NATURE.**

I dwell . . . with him who has a contrite and humble spirit.

ISAIAH 57:15

rom an unknown source comes an article titled, "How
To Be Miserable." It says, "Think about yourself. Talk about
yourself. Use 'I' as often as possible. Mirror yourself continually in the
opinion of others. Listen greedily to what people say about you.
Expect to be appreciated. Be suspicious. Be jealous and envious.
Be sensitive to slights. Never forgive a criticism. Trust nobody but
yourself. Insist on consideration and respect. Demand agreement with
your own views on everything. Sulk if people are not grateful to you
for favors shown them. Never forget a service you have rendered.
Shirk your duties if you can. Do as little as possible for others."

Seeing ourselves as the center of the universe leads to misery.
We weren't made to be the focus of our own attention. We were made
to give our hearts to "the High and Lofty One," who lives with those
who have a contrite and humble spirit. —M. R. D. II

A PERSON IS NEVER SO EMPTY AS WHEN HE IS FULL OF SELF.

*The floods came, and the winds blew
and beat on that house; and it fell.*

MATTHEW 7:27

I grew up near the shores of Lake Michigan and always loved the sand dunes. Nothing was more fun than to scramble up their steep slopes through the loose sand. Each step up a 300-foot dune was followed by a half-step slide back down. But the view of the sparkling waves from the top made the climb worthwhile. Other people loved that view as well, and they built beautiful homes on the crests of the dunes. I often thought how wonderful it would be to live in one of those homes.

Then several years ago the lake's water level began to rise. Soon the beach was gone. Howling gales sent huge waves crashing against the dunes. The sand began to erode and gradually it was pulled out into the lake by the returning waves. As the dunes were eaten away, many of those beautiful houses came crashing down.

That's the way it is in life. When the storms of disappointment and heartache come, we need to rest our souls on the solid foundation of Jesus Christ. —D. C. E.

**JESUS IS NO SECURITY AGAINST LIFE'S STORMS,
BUT HE IS PERFECT SECURITY IN LIFE'S STORMS.**

I have been crucified with Christ; it is no longer I who live, but Christ lives in me.

GALATIANS 2:20

Countless icebergs float in the frigid waters around Greenland. Some are tiny; others tower skyward. At times the small ones move in one direction while their gigantic counterparts go in another. The small ones are subject to surface winds, but the huge ice masses are carried along by deep ocean currents.

Our lives are subject to two similar forces. The winds represent everything changeable, unpredictable, distressing. But simultaneous with these adverse gusts or gales is another force more powerful than anything on the surface. It's the sure movement of God's purposes and the deep flow of His unchanging love. It's in that unseen current that we must rest the destiny of our souls.

As we keep trusting the Lord, the surface winds won't move us. Rather, we'll be carried along with the deep current of God's love and power. —D. J. D.

BENEATH THE RESTLESS SURFACE OF LIFE, FLOW GOD'S LOVE AND POWER.

Keep your heart with all diligence.

PROVERBS 4:23

Ever try painting a room without spattering paint on yourself? Or playing ball without getting dirty? Or washing the car without getting wet? It's hard, isn't it?

How about living in modern society and staying "unspotted from the world"? (James 1:27). Ever try it? That's the goal James set out for us in his epistle.

Here is a five-point evil-avoidance strategy from the fourth chapter of Proverbs that can help:

1. Make wisdom your life's goal (v. 20–22).
2. Guard your heart against evil (v. 23).
3. Never speak deceitfully (v. 24).
4. Keep your eyes on what is good and pure (v. 25).
5. Keep your feet from evil ways (vv. 26–27).

Let's ask God each day to guide our steps and guard our hearts.

—J. D. B.

**WE EITHER LEAVE OUR MARK ON THE WORLD
OR THE WORLD LEAVES ITS MARK ON US.**

But to him who does not work but believes on Him . . . ,
his faith is accounted for righteousness.

ROMANS 4:5

I read about an instant cake mix that was a big flop. The instructions said all you had to do was add water and bake. The company couldn't understand why it didn't sell—until their research discovered that the buying public felt uneasy about a mix that required only water. Apparently people thought it was too easy. So the company altered the formula and changed the directions to call for adding an egg to the mix in addition to the water. The idea worked and sales jumped dramatically.

That story reminds me of how some people react to the plan of salvation. To them it sounds too easy and simple to be true, even though the Bible says, "By grace you have been saved through faith . . . ; it is the gift of God, not of works" (Eph. 2:8–9). They feel that there is something they must add to God's "recipe" for salvation. They think they must perform good works to gain God's favor. But the Bible is clear—we are saved, "not by works of righteousness which we have done, but according to His mercy" (Titus 3:5). —*R. W. D.*

WE ARE SAVED BY GOD'S MERCY, NOT BY OUR MERIT.

They are not of the world, just as I am not of the world.

JOHN 17:16

The water spider is an amazing little creature. Called the frogman of the spider world, it lives in rivers and streams. How does this fascinating species survive in its watery environment? It spins a tough basket-like web of silk, a kind of diving bell, and anchors it under water to plants or other objects. Then it captures a surface air bubble, which it pulls down and ejects into its underwater house, filling it with air. This combination of web building and bubble trapping allows the water spider to live in an environment that normally would destroy it.

As Christians, we too live in an environment that could destroy us. The world's values, attitudes, and practices threaten to drown us unless we are able to protect ourselves from them. How are we to survive spiritually in this hostile, worldly environment? We must build a "bubble" of protection around ourselves by studying the Scriptures, praying, fellowshiping with believers, communing with the Holy Spirit, trusting God, and obeying His Word. —D. C. E.

WE CAN BE IN THE WORLD WITHOUT THE WORLD BEING IN US.

They cry out to the LORD . . . , and He
brings them out of their distresses.

PSALM 107:28

In 1983 I watched one of the America's Cup yacht races as the ships competed off the coast of Rhode Island. Through my binoculars I could observe the yachts *Liberty* and *Australia II* as they raced for the prestigious championship. Although the boats were basically the same size, there was a marked difference between them. The heavier *Liberty* sailed best under winds of 15 to 20 knots. The *Australia II*, with her innovative super-keel, performed better in winds between 7 and 12 knots. Yet, no matter what conditions the crews faced, they each took full advantage of the available wind and competed with great skill.

As I watched, I thought, Christians should react like that to life's trying situations. Some people make the best progress when the sailing is not too rough, while others require the strong winds of adversity to develop their character. In either case, the key is to adjust to the conditions with God's help. —P. R. V.

YOU CANNOT DIRECT THE WIND, BUT YOU CAN ADJUST YOUR SAILS.

*I also count all things loss for the excellence
of the knowledge of Christ Jesus my Lord.*

PHILIPPIANS 3:8

The airline had mangled Debbie's luggage. Then her purse disappeared. Instead of entering the airport through an enclosed corridor, she stumbled off the plane in the pouring rain. She was drenched, far from home with no money, no identification, and no dry clothes.

Under normal conditions Debbie would have been furious, but that night it didn't matter. She had just survived the crash of Flight 1420 in Little Rock, Arkansas. "When I walked off that plane," Debbie said, "I walked off with nothing, then I stopped and thought, I have everything." She had suddenly realized that her life was more important than all she had lost.

It sometimes takes a dramatic turn of events to alter our perspective. That was true for Saul of Tarsus. He had treasured his hard-earned reputation for "righteousness" more than anything in the world (Phil. 3:4–6). But when he met Christ on the Damascus road (Acts 9:1–6), his whole outlook changed. Later he wrote, "What things were gain to me, these I have counted loss for Christ" (Phil. 3:7).

—D. C. M.

WHEN WE HAVE NOTHING LEFT BUT CHRIST, WE FIND HE IS ENOUGH.

I thank God—through Jesus Christ our Lord!

ROMANS 7:25

A monk who had a quick temper was known to "pass the buck" for his fits of anger—always blaming his fellow monastery residents. So he decided to move to a place of absolute solitude in a desert, thinking that if he got away from the others he could be victorious.

One morning he accidentally knocked over a pitcher of water. A few minutes later he bumped it again, and once more it fell on its side and spilled its contents. Losing his temper, the monk picked up the pitcher and hurled it to the ground. As it broke into smithereens, the truth hit him: he couldn't blame others for his flare-ups. The real trouble was within him.

How true of all of us! The apostle Paul was keenly aware of the outworking of sin in his life. He cried, "O wretched man that I am! Who will deliver me from this body of death?" (Rom. 7:24). But he was confident of final victory, for he answered his own question, saying, "I thank God—through Jesus Christ our Lord!" —R. W. D.

THE HEART OF THE PROBLEM IS THE PROBLEM OF OUR HEART.

Fear the Lᴏʀᴅ and depart from evil.

Pʀᴏᴠᴇʀʙs 3:7-8

It was only a little comma, but it cost the Lockheed corporation millions of dollars! An error was made in a contract with an international customer—a misplaced comma in a crucial number. The company insisted that the manufacturer honor the contract as written. Unfortunately for Lockheed, the error was made in an equation that adjusted the sales price, and it cost them $70 million.

That's the way it is with sin too. It has a high cost, even though at the time it may seem so small. Seemingly harmless transgressions can end up doing great damage. Proverbs 3 tells us that we can expect God's chastening if we disobey Him (vv. 11–12). That's why we would be wise to "fear the Lord and depart from evil" (v. 7). If we take God and His Word seriously, we will hate any sin in our lives—big or little. —D. C. E.

Uᴘʀᴏᴏᴛ ᴛʜᴇ ᴡᴇᴇᴅ ᴏꜰ sɪɴ ᴡʜɪʟᴇ ɪᴛ's sᴛɪʟʟ sᴍᴀʟʟ.

If anyone serves Me, let him follow Me.

JOHN 12:26

The sign alongside the road in England said, "Changed Priorities Ahead."

When I asked the taxi driver what it meant, he said, "It has to do with how you give way to the traffic in the roundabout just ahead. You yield to a different driver than usual."

Long after we negotiated the traffic circle, I continued to ponder the sign. I saw it as a vivid three-word summary of what it means to follow Christ.

When Jesus called Peter and Andrew to be His disciples, "they immediately left their nets and followed Him" (Matt. 4:20). At that moment, it was as if God placed this sign on the road of their lives: *Changed Priorities Ahead.* He does the same in our lives as we hear Christ calling us to follow Him.

When we follow Jesus Christ, we discover that changed priorities are necessary to negotiate the road ahead. —D. C. M.

WHEN WE FOLLOW CHRIST, OUR WHOLE LIFE CHANGES DIRECTION.

In Him we live and move and have our being.

ACTS 17:28

Russian peasant farmers enjoy telling the story of the day a commissar came to a farmer and inquired about the year's potato crop. "Oh, it was wonderful," replied the farmer. "Good, good," said the official. "Just how big was it?" "Oh, it was so big it reached up to the very foot of God." The commissar's countenance changed. With a scowl, he said, "But comrade, this is a communist state and we are atheists. You must not forget, there is no God!" "That's right, commissar that's what I mean. No God—no potatoes."

A deep truth lies hidden in this humorous tale. God is the source of all things. Without Him, we could not draw a single breath, our bodies could not function, and we would have no provision for our daily sustenance.

Athiests may have convinced themselves that God does not exist. Yet we who are His children know otherwise. —D. C. E.

DIVINE RESOURCES ARE NEVER EXHAUSTED.

How shall they hear without a preacher?

ROMANS 10:14

ohn Harper, a Scottish minister, was traveling by ship to preach for 3 months at Moody Church in Chicago. As the ship crossed the Atlantic, it struck an iceberg and began to sink. Some passengers were able to reach lifeboats, but many, Harper included, were flung into the cold Atlantic.

As the people frantically tried to stay afloat, Harper swam around asking individuals if they knew Jesus. At one point, Harper approached a passenger floating on a piece of debris and pleaded with him to trust Christ. Just before Harper slipped under the icy waters for the last time, he said, "Believe on the Lord Jesus Christ, and thou shalt be saved."

Four years later, at a meeting of survivors of that ship, the Titanic, the man testified that he had been saved twice that night. First, he had trusted Christ because of Harper's witness, and second, he had been plucked from the frigid sea. —J. D. B.

WE NEED TO TELL EVERYONE ABOUT THE ONE WHO CAN SAVE ANYONE.

Make a joyful shout to God, all the earth!

PSALM 66:1

As I stood on a lakeshore one summer holiday and saw the hundreds and hundreds of people boating, swimming, picnicking, or simply walking together, I thought of the value of celebrating important events together with friends and loved ones.

Did you ever try to celebrate something alone? A fireworks display isn't much fun if there's no one to "ooooh and aaaah" with. Picnics need people. Birthdays, anniversaries, graduations—they all go better with lots of friends and relatives around.

As Christians, we have much to celebrate—and not alone or just a few times a year! We can meet regularly with others who follow Christ, to encourage one another in love and good works (Heb. 10:24–25), and to celebrate the goodness of the Lord. The psalmist encourages us to recall "the works of God" and lift our voices in praise to Him (Ps. 66:5–8). —J. D. B.

IF YOU KNOW CHRIST, YOU ALWAYS HAVE A REASON TO CELEBRATE.

The Word of God is living and powerful.

HEBREWS 4:12

Author Ronald B. Schwartz asked scores of well-known contemporary writers to name the books that influenced them most deeply. Their responses ranged from the novels of Dostoevsky to the popular stories of Mark Twain. The works of Dickens, Shakespeare, and Faulkner were mentioned many times. But topping the list was the Bible. Why?

Perhaps because most writers want to deal with the "big questions" of life, and the Bible is the ultimate book for life's big questions: Who am I? Why am I here? Is there a God? Does life have any meaning or purpose?

The pages of Scripture bring us face to face with ourselves, with God, and with His grand design for our lives. The Bible, according to the late journalist Malcolm Muggeridge, is "the book that reads me." —D. C. M.

THE BIBLE IS GOD'S ANSWER BOOK.

*Comfort the fainthearted, uphold
the weak, be patient with all.*

1 THESSALONIANS 5:14

During the Boer War (1899–1902), a man was convicted of a very unusual crime. He was found guilty of being a "discourager." The South African town of Ladysmith was under attack, and this traitor would move up and down the lines of soldiers who were defending the city and do everything he could to discourage them. He would point out the enemy's strength, the difficulty of defending against them, and the inevitable capture of the city. He didn't use a gun in his attack. It wasn't necessary. His weapon was the power of discouragement.

Encouragement, on the other hand, can be a powerful friend. It strengthens the weak, imparts courage to the fainthearted, and gives hope to the faltering. One of the greatest ministries we can have is to lift the spirits of fellow believers.

Encourage someone today! —R. W. D.

A LITTLE ENCOURAGEMENT CAN SPARK A GREAT ACCOMPLISHMENT.

Let them do good, that they be rich in good
works, ready to give, willing to share.

1 TIMOTHY 6:18

businessman who sold his road construction company stunned his employees by dividing a third of the profit among them. Each of his 550 workers received a share of the $128 million, with some of his long-term associates getting bonuses of $1 million each—tax free.

"It's sharing good times, that's really all it is," the owner said. "People work exceedingly hard for us. . . . I wanted to go out doing the right thing."

It's easy to say, "Well, if I had millions of dollars, I'd be happy to share what I have with others." But would I? What riches of time, talent, or treasure am I hoarding today? What has God given me that I am unwilling to share?

In whatever way God blesses us, He longs for us to be joyful and generous as we pass it on. —D. C. M.

THE LORD SEES HOW MUCH WE GIVE AND HOW MUCH WE KEEP.

Father, keep . . . those whom You have given
Me, that they may be one as We are.

JOHN 17:11

Mike Barker told me that the obstacle course in Air Force basic training changed his life. On his first attempt he completed the course far ahead of everyone else, but he was immediately confronted by his drill sergeant, who demanded, "Where are all your buddies?" "Back there, sir," Mike replied. "I won!"

The sergeant barked, "The obstacle course isn't about coming in first! It's about finishing! Everybody finishes or nobody wins. Go back and run it again, and this time help the guys who are struggling along the way!" That began Mike's transformation from a lone competitor obsessed with winning into an encourager whose goal was to build teamwork.

Jesus didn't move through life as a solitary figure. As He neared the cross, He poured out His heart in prayer for His disciples: "Holy Father, keep through Your name those whom You have given Me. . . . While I was with them in the world, I kept them in Your name" (John 17:11–12). Now that's teamwork! —D. C. M.

WHEN WE WORK TOGETHER, WE DIVIDE
THE EFFORT AND MULTIPLY THE EFFECT.

There is laid up for me the crown of righteousness.

2 TIMOTHY 4:8

In the mid-1970s, Ed Roberts created the world's first commercially successful personal computer (PC). He hired a nineteen-year-old named Bill Gates to write software for him.

Roberts sold his computer business in 1977 and bought a farm. Seven years later, at the age of 41, he entered medical school. Today Bill Gates is the head of the largest software company in the world. Ed Roberts is a physician in a small Georgia town. Roberts says, "The implication is that the PC is the most important thing I've ever done, and I don't think that's true. Every day I deal with things that are equally if not more important here with my patients."

How can we evaluate the significance of our lives? Something deep inside tells us it cannot be measured by wealth and fame. The apostle Paul approached the end of life with a peaceful sense of successful completion. He wrote, "I have fought the good fight, I have finished the race, I have kept the faith" (2 Tim. 4:7). —D. C. M.

**THE MEASURE OF A LIFE IS DETERMINED
BY THE RULER OF THE UNIVERSE.**

Tremble, O earth, at the presence of the LORD.

PSALM 114:7

*B*ack and forth, back and forth go the pounding waves of the sea. From ages past, the continents have been separated by the mighty oceans. Man has learned to travel over them, to descend to the bottom of them, and to travel through them—but their immensity and the relentless force of their waves remain untamable. Rocks are crushed, shorelines are changed, and even experienced sailors can be driven aground or sent to the bottom of the sea. The combined genius of man and the most powerful equipment can do little to conquer the oceans.

But the seas are no problem for God. Psalm 114 refers to the parting of the Red Sea (Exod. 14:13–31) to describe God's great power. The psalmist wrote, "The sea saw it and fled" (Ps. 114:3). Then he asked, "What ails you, O sea, that you fled?" (v. 5). The answer is implied: The seas were obeying the command of God. —D. C. E.

**THE POWER OF GOD WITHIN YOU IS
GREATER THAN THE PRESSURE AROUND YOU.**

*Let us lay aside every weight, and the
sin which so easily ensnares us.*

HEBREWS 12:1

A former commander of the Imperial Russian Navy said that he went to London during World War I for training. There he learned how to fly one of three dirigibles that Russia had bought from England.

But first he had to learn to fly a balloon. He recalled getting into the gondola and seeing all four sides covered with sandbags. To begin the ascent, sand was released until the huge balloon slowly lifted off the ground. As more sand went over the side, the craft ascended higher.

The man then applied this to our relationship with the Lord: "Now that I'm a Christian, I understand that when God begins to clean up my heart, I get closer and closer to Him."

Selfish attitudes, besetting sins, and worldly cares keep us from getting off the ground spiritually. But when we lay them aside, we experience the uplifting joy of fellowship with the Father. —M. R. D. II

**IF YOU'RE NOT AS CLOSE TO GOD AS
YOU USED TO BE, GUESS WHO MOVED.**

God is Spirit, and those who worship
Him must worship in spirit and truth.

JOHN 4:24

What color is God? That's the question James McBride, an African-American author and musician, asked his Jewish mother when he was a boy. His autobiography contains the following story: Walking home from church one day, he asked her if God was black or white. She replied, "God is not black. God is not white. God is the color of water. Water doesn't have a color." That was indeed a wise response.

We know that God doesn't have a color because He doesn't have a body. He is Spirit and He's present everywhere (Ps. 139:7–12). Whether we're sitting at home or flying miles above the earth, He is there and we can call out to Him. His ears are always open to our cry (Ps. 34:15). He isn't an idol or a mere idea. God is Spirit, almighty, always present, ever available. —V. C. G.

OUR GREATEST PRIVILEGE IS TO ENJOY GOD'S PRESENCE.

*As you did it to one of the least of these
My brethren, you did it to Me.*

MATTHEW 25:40

A young man strolling along a beach at dawn stopped to watch an older man pick up starfish and toss them back into the sea. The older man said he was rescuing the starfish before the hot summer sun could bake them. Sarcastically, the young man said, "There must be hundreds of starfish here. How can you make any difference?" The old gentleman looked at the starfish in his hand before throwing it into the waves. "It makes a big difference to this one," he replied.

Jesus never let the vast crowds discourage Him from helping individuals. In Luke 8 we read that a multitude pressed about Him (v. 40), yet He took time to minister to one man and one woman in need (vv. 41–56). Jesus calls us to do the same. —J. E. Y.

**DO WHAT YOU CAN TO HELP ONE AT
A TIME AND LEAVE THE REST TO GOD.**

You have been grieved by various trials, that . . . your faith, being much more precious than gold . . . may be found to praise.

1 PETER 1:6–7

In the 1980s, Northern Nevada was the site of a gold strike. The discovery would have been beyond the imagination of 19th-century prospectors, for the gold in those western hills is virtually invisible. Even after being magnified 1,500 times, most of the particles remain imperceptible.

Modern technology, however, has found a way to extract the gold. First, tons of ore are crushed to the consistency of fine sand. Then cyanide is added to dissolve the granules into a clear solution. When zinc dust is blended in, the gold separates from the mixture. The gold was there all the time, but it couldn't be seen.

There's a similarity here to life's troubles. You may not see in them the rich potential of a strong faith, but it's there. To have it developed is much more precious than gold! —M. R. D. II

FAITH-TESTING TIMES CAN BE FAITH-STRENGTHENING TIMES.

I will pray the Father, and He will give you another Helper.

JOHN 14:16

A few years ago, a 42-foot sailboat got caught in stormy seas off the east coast of the United States. Waves rose higher and higher until a giant wave flipped the boat upside down. The heavy keel righted the craft, but damage was significant.

A Coast Guard cutter quickly responded to the sailboat's SOS. But when the ship located the desperate boat, no one could be rescued because of the violent seas. So the cutter drew as close as possible to the smaller craft, taking the brunt of the waves. The ship remained alongside the imperiled boat throughout the storm and then led her safely into port.

The action of this Coast Guard cutter is an illustration of the ministry of the Holy Spirit. Jesus told His disciples in John 14:16, "I will pray the Father, and He will give you another Helper." The word *Helper* may also be translated "Comforter" or "Counselor," and literally means "one called alongside to help." The Holy Spirit guides and protects us through life's storms, much like that rescue ship escorted the sailboat. —D. C. E.

GOD'S SPIRIT LIVES INSIDE US AND WALKS BESIDE US.

God has set the members . . . in the body just as He pleased.

1 CORINTHIANS 12:18

The honeybee has one of the most highly developed social structures in the animal kingdom. At the heart of the hive, which may house as many as 80,000 bees, is the queen. Without her, the colony has no future. But the 80,000 don't just sit around watching their queen. Each bee has a specialized duty to fulfill.

The forager bees encounter the perils of the outside world to collect food. The guard bees protect the hive entrance from intruders. The undertakers are responsible for removing dead bodies from the hive. The water collectors bring in moisture to regulate humidity. The plasterers make a kind of cement to repair the hive. The variety and specialization of the worker bees seem endless.

In a similar way, the Lord has given special gifts and tasks to all the people in His church. No one has been called merely to sit around. Everyone can do something. The work of the church will not get done unless all of us do what God has called us to do. —M. R. D. II

THE CHURCH WORKS BEST WITH PARTICIPANTS, NOT SPECTATORS.

God also has . . . given Him the name which is above every name.

PHILIPPIANS 2:9

What's in a name? Plenty, according to Justin Kaplan and Anne Bernays, authors of the book *The Language of Names*. In the section of their book where they discuss literary names, Kaplan and Bernays point out that English novelist Charles Dickens was a great master at naming his characters. Seth Pecksniff, Wilkins Micawber, Tiny Tim, Sir Mulberry Hawk, and Thomas Gradgrind are just a few examples of characters whose names reflect who they are.

For Christians, the name above all other names is Jesus. What's in that name? All the grace of God, all the wonder of redemption, all that we believe, and all that we are hoping for. We say it, we sing it, and adoration fills our souls. We anticipate the indescribable glory of that day when every knee will bow and every tongue, by glad choice or by divine constraint, will praise that highest and holiest of all names—Jesus! —V. C. G.

**THE NAME OF JESUS IS PROFANITY TO THE SINNER
BUT HEAVEN'S PASSWORD TO THE SAINT.**

It is good for me that I have been
afflicted, that I may learn Your statutes.

PSALM 119:71

Have you heard about the "gator aid" that was given to enlisted men in a Florida training camp during World War II? The daily training for those GIs included a run through an obstacle course. On the final stretch of the endurance test, they had to grab a rope and swing across a broad, shallow pool.

Under the blazing sun the water looked so inviting to the men that most of them soon developed a habit of making it only halfway across the pond—that is, until an enterprising lieutenant made it the new home for a large alligator. From that day on, the recruits left the ground 15 feet from the water's edge and fell sprawling in the dust on the other side.

Likewise, our behavior as Christians must sometimes be shaped by the "encouragement" of unfavorable circumstances. Without God's loving correction and faithful discipline we would never develop spiritual strength and endurance. —M. R. D. II

LIFE'S CHALLENGES ARE DESIGNED NOT TO
BREAK US, BUT TO BEND US TOWARD GOD.

The Lord knows those who are His.

2 TIMOTHY 2:19

The guillemot is a small Arctic seabird that lives on the rocky cliffs of northern coastal regions. These birds flock together by the thousands in comparatively small areas.

Because of the crowded conditions, hundreds of females lay their pear-shaped eggs side by side in a long row on a narrow ledge. Since the eggs all look alike, it's incredible that a mother bird can identify those that belong to her. Yet studies show that she knows her own eggs so well even when one is moved, she finds it and returns it to its original location. She is never confused.

The Bible tells us that the heavenly Father intimately understands each of His children. He knows their every thought and emotion, and is "acquainted with all [their] ways" (Ps. 139:3). From morning till night He gives personal attention to all their circumstances. They are well-loved and well-known. —M. R. D. II

WITH GOD, NO ONE IS EVER LOST IN A CROWD!

A little folding of the hands to rest;
so shall your poverty come like a prowler.

PROVERBS 24:33–34

*S*omeday I'm going to write a book called *How to Have a Crummy Lawn.* All the pages will be blank because that's what is required—nothing. Just leave it alone and in no time dandelions will sprout, crabgrass will spread, and weeds with Latin names will thrive where the lawn used to be. The magic formula for a bad lawn is no water, no fertilizer, no weed killer, no care.

The book, of course, will be immensely unpopular because no one wants a crummy lawn, not consciously at least. They end up with one, though, simply through neglect.

When I'm out digging dandelions, I often ask myself if I'm putting as much time and effort into maintaining my spiritual life as I am my lawn. How easily the weeds of anger and discouragement take root in my soul. How quickly anxiety crowds out peace in my heart. The formula for a bad lawn and a bad life are exactly the same—all it takes is a little neglect. —D. C. M.

NEGLECT IS ALL IT TAKES TO RUIN A LIFE.

I love the LORD, because He has heard my voice.

PSALM 116:1

E-mail. In case you're not familiar with this trendy buzzword, it refers to correspondence that is transmitted over computer networks. Whenever I click the SEND NOW command on my computer to zip a message along the cyberspace network, I always worry, "Is my e-mail actually getting to its destination? Will I get a response?"

You may have had those same questions in another realm of communication—prayer. But there are some important differences. For my e-mail to arrive, my equipment and my programs must function correctly. Prayer, on the other hand, is just me talking to God, with no chance of a glitch.

If I haven't clogged the lines with sin, my prayers will always be heard (Ps. 66:18; 3:4). And when I do sin, God is waiting to forgive (1 John 1:9). With e-mail, my message could sit unread for days. Not so with prayer. God is always there (Ps. 6:9). And although I may never get a response to some e-mail messages, with God the answers will always come. —J. D. B.

YOU'LL NEVER GET A BUSY SIGNAL ON THE PRAYER LINE TO HEAVEN.

"Well done, good servant."

LUKE 19:17

The story is told of a man visiting a farmer who was going through hard times. He wondered what had gone wrong, so he asked the farmer, "Did you have a poor harvest this year?" The response quickly came back, "I didn't have any!"

"Oh, I'm sorry," his friend sympathized. "Didn't you even get corn?" "No, and I didn't plant any. I was afraid we wouldn't get enough rain."

"Well, what about your potatoes?" He exclaimed, "I decided not to plant any because I was afraid the bugs would get them."

No wonder this man didn't reap a harvest! Which reminds me of the unfaithful servant who was punished for his failure to make good use of the money entrusted to him. Because of fear, he put it away "in a handkerchief" (Luke 19:20). He played it safe—and lost.

Let's seek God's will in prayer and then dare to do as He commands! —R. W. D.

DON'T MAKE A CEMETERY OF YOUR LIFE BY BURYING YOUR TALENTS.

God is our refuge and strength, a very present help in trouble.

PSALM 46:1

The safest place in South Florida during the hurricane season may be the National Hurricane Center in Miami. The $5 million structure boasts 10-inch concrete walls designed to withstand the force of 130 mph winds. Because the fierce storms come every year, the Center is there to provide a safe working environment for the people who monitor the weather and issue the warnings. When other residents leave, they must stay.

Just like hurricanes, the storms of our lives arrive with unnerving regularity. Often they strike without warning and linger without welcome, testing the limits of our faith and endurance. But God Himself is our center of safety. It is not our strength but His that shields us from the whirling winds of circumstance and change.

—D. C. M.

WHEN TROUBLE BLOWS INTO YOUR LIFE, SEEK SHELTER IN GOD.

*Cornelius [was] a devout man and one
who feared God with all his household.*

ACTS 10:1–2

A prominent senator was dropped from the "Green Book"—the list of Washington societal elite who are invited to special functions. Why? Because he never attended the events. Instead, he went home each night to be with his family.

Then he discovered he had cancer. A difficult career choice faced him. The night before he announced his decision not to run for office again, he said to his wife, "You know, the only thing I'll probably ever be remembered for is that I loved my wife." To which she replied, "And what's wrong with that?"

Families that are built on love, respect, and togetherness instead of social climbing or the pursuit of successful careers are a nation's hope for survival. And when their values reflect a love for Jesus Christ, they hold a special place in God's plan for the world. —D. J. D.

A NATION IS ONLY AS STRONG AS ITS FAMILIES.

He who waters will also be watered himself.

PROVERBS 11:25

visitor to a lighthouse said to the keeper, "Aren't you afraid to live here with the storms and high winds constantly lashing the walls?"

"Oh, we have to be more concerned about those out on the sea," the man replied. "We think only of having our lamps burning brightly and keeping the reflectors clear so that those in greater danger may be saved."

We too are to be more concerned about others than we are about ourselves (Phil. 2:3–4). Generosity and selflessness produce an abundant life of joy and rich reward. According to the Scriptures, if we give freely to others, we will receive abundant blessing.

As we focus our attention on giving refreshing help to the needy, we will be refreshed by the Lord. —H. G. B.

**SERVICE IS WORKING AND GIVING,
AND NOT REGRETTING THE COST.**

The eternal God is your refuge, and
underneath are the everlasting arms.

DEUTERONOMY 33:27

A mother eagle builds a comfortable nest for her young, padding it with feathers from her own breast. But the God-given instinct that builds that secure nest also forces the eaglets out of it before long. Eagles are made to fly, and love will not fail to teach them. Only then will they become what they are meant to be.

So one day the mother eagle will disturb the twigs of the nest, making it an uncomfortable place to stay. Then she will pick up a perplexed eaglet, soar into the sky, and drop it. The little bird will begin to free-fall. Where is Mama now? She is not far away. Quickly she will swoop under and catch the fledgling on one strong wing. She will repeat this exercise until each eaglet is capable of flying on its own.

Are you afraid of free-falling? Remember, God will fly to your rescue and spread His everlasting arms beneath you. He will also teach you something new and wonderful through it. Falling into God's arms is nothing to be afraid of. —J. E. Y.

GOD'S LOVE DOES NOT KEEP US FROM
TRIALS BUT SEES US THROUGH THEM.

Happy are the people whose God is the LORD!

PSALM 144:15

What's the world's happiest nation? A Time magazine article reports that pollsters have tried to find a definitive answer to that question—but without success.

Despite claims to the contrary, a 1992 Gallup survey pronounced France "among the unhappiest societies on the Continent."

A survey in Germany found that "less than one-third admitted to being 'very happy.'"

Still another poll disclosed that among the inhabitants of Great Britain, "Fifty-four percent feel their country is a snobbish, class-ridden society." When asked if they would like to leave the country, "Forty-seven percent said they would pack their bags before teatime."

Genuine happiness—a mood of contentment, joy, and hope—doesn't depend on the country one lives in. It depends on a right relationship with God. Geography and race don't determine membership in God's family. Faith in Jesus Christ determines that. —V. C. G.

TRUE HAPPINESS COMES FROM KNOWING GOD.

Follow Me, and I will make you become fishers of men.

MARK 1:17

Okay, I admit it. I like to fish. No, I'm not the buy-the-latest-bass-boat, get-out-every-weekend kind of guy. But I enjoy fishing for walleyes at a nearby dam in the summer or catching perch through the ice on one of Michigan's many lakes in winter.

That makes me interested in things related to fishing. So I was hooked when I saw this bumper sticker on the back of an old pickup truck:

Life's Short: Fish Hard

I chuckled, but the more I thought about it the more I was caught by this idea: As a follower of Jesus Christ, I am a "fisher of men." I have been commanded by the Lord Jesus to proclaim the gospel message (Matt. 28:19–20), to tell others about the wonderful, saving love of God for all people.

Yes, life is short. So, as obedient followers of Jesus Christ, let's "fish hard" to bring others to Him. —D. C. E.

IT'S NEVER OUT OF SEASON TO FISH FOR SOULS.

*Not forsaking the assembling of ourselves
together, as is the manner of some.*

HEBREWS 10:25

Josef Gabor grew up in Czechoslovakia when it was
dominated by communism, and religion was despised as
weakness. His father taught communist doctrine classes. But
Josef's mother, who believed in Jesus Christ, took Josef and his brother
with her to church.

They got up early each Sunday morning and took a 3-hour
train ride to Prague. Then they walked to the church and sat through a
2 1/2-hour service. After eating lunch in a nearby park, they returned
to church for another 2 1/2-hour meeting. Then they took the 3-hour
ride home.

Today Josef Gabor is a missionary to his own people in
Czechoslovakia. When he tells about going to church as a child, his
eyes fill with tears of gratitude for a mother who cared enough about
his spiritual welfare to help him come to know and serve Christ.
—D. C. E.

GO TO CHURCH IF YOU WANT TO GROW IN CHRIST.

When my spirit was overwhelmed
within me, then You knew my path.

PSALM 142:3

Years ago a tourist was being shown through one of the oldest castles in England. He admired the rich furnishings, the valuable art treasures, and the ornate carvings. Then he noticed a strange tapestry that had a wild, irregular pattern of color and knotted threads. The guide, seeing the man's quizzical look, said, "That's actually the most beautiful piece of art in the castle, but we regularly turn its face to the wall to protect the delicate colors from the light." Carefully turning over the weaving, he showed the tourist the most exquisite tapestry he had ever seen.

So too, sometimes God in His wisdom turns the tapestry of our life so that all its beautiful colors and pleasing patterns are hidden from view. When this happens, we must not despair, for God knows what He's doing. He recognizes that too much of the sunlight of carefree days and prosperity would fade our testimony and ruin His design. In His time, He will change our circumstances so that the beauty and symmetry of His all-wise purposes will again be evident.
—H. G. B.

GOD USES LIFE'S REVERSES TO MOVE US FORWARD.

Be strong in the Lord and in the power of His might.

EPHESIANS 6:10

The army of Alexander the Great was advancing on Persia. At one critical point, it appeared that his troops might be defeated. The soldiers had taken so much plunder from their previous campaigns that they had become weighted down and were losing their effectiveness in combat. Alexander immediately commanded that all the spoils be thrown into a heap and burned. The men complained bitterly but soon came to see the wisdom of the order. Someone wrote, "It was as if wings had been given to them—they walked lightly again." Victory was assured.

As soldiers of Christ, we must rid ourselves of anything that would hinder us in the conflict with our spiritual enemy. To win, we must "lay aside every weight" that would drag us down and rob us of our strength and endurance. The watchword must be: Off with the weight! —R. W. D.

**THROW OFF THE WEIGHT OF THE
WORLD BEFORE IT DRAGS YOU DOWN.**

August

[We are] justified freely by His grace.

ROMANS 3:24

Everywhere you turn today, you see advertising. Billboards shout and T-shirts tout their messages. Radio spots, TV commercials, and newspaper ads make urgent pitches. *Adweek* columnist Barbara Lippert looked the situation over and remarked, "Everything in America is a product being sold—whether it's a celebrity, a television show, whether it's anything."

Of course, we know that the goods and services being advertised carry a price tag. We have to pay for what is being offered. No one expects to get something for nothing. There is, however, one huge exception. When God decided to offer something as amazing and wonderful as eternal life, He chose to pay the price Himself in Christ.

Each year people respond to ads and spend millions of dollars on soft drinks, cars, pizza, and carpet. But the best offer ever made carries no price tag. It is not for sale. —J. D. B.

SALVATION IS FREE BECAUSE CHRIST PAID THE INFINITE PRICE.

None of these things move me . . . ,
so that I may finish my race with joy.

ACTS 20:24

About 200 years ago in England there lived a great humanitarian named Jonas Hanway. In his travels in foreign countries, he had discovered the usefulness of what was then the little-known umbrella. He decided to introduce it to England, believing it would be readily accepted.

Many people poked fun at him, however, and young boys often pelted him with cabbages and rotten eggs because they considered him peculiar. Hanway never let this stop him, even though he was ridiculed for 30 years as "the umbrella man." Eventually people recognized the usefulness of the umbrella, and today few would want to be without one.

A spiritual parallel to this story is found in the perseverance and faithfulness of the apostle Paul. That "ambassador in chains" was kept in cruel Roman dungeons and endured terrible persecution; yet he confidently declared that none of these things moved him. In spite of all opposition, he clung to the truth of the gospel, which the Lord had commissioned him to proclaim to the world. —H. G. B.

GREAT ENDURANCE IS ESSENTIAL TO GREAT ACHIEVEMENT.

I love Your commandments more than gold, yes, than fine gold!

PSALM 119:127

An elderly woman in Scotland lived in abject poverty. Many years earlier, her son had left to live in America and had not returned to visit. One day a friend inquired, "Does your son ever help you?" Reluctantly she admitted, "No, but he writes me nice long letters and sends me interesting pictures."

The friend wanted to speak harshly of the man, but he held back and simply asked, "May I see the pictures?" The woman took them out of a drawer, and to the friend's amazement they were all sizable banknotes. Through the years she had been needlessly living in poverty.

Many Christians are like that. They exist as spiritual paupers while possessing unlimited wealth. By failing to read and study the Scriptures, they neglect to cash in on their treasures.

It's up to us. We can neglect God's Word or we can appropriate its riches by studying it and letting God's Spirit teach us. —P. R. V.

**MANY PEOPLE PUT THEIR BIBLE ON THE
SHELF INSTEAD OF IN THEIR HEARTS.**

Do not worry about tomorrow. . . .
Sufficient for the day is its own trouble.

MATTHEW 6:34

The story is told about a man whose store was destroyed by fire. And to make matters worse, he had failed to renew his fire insurance. Later that day, an old friend asked how he was coping with the shocking loss. The answer was both surprising and pleasing. "I'm getting along just fine," he said. "I had breakfast this morning, and it isn't time to eat again."

With a thankful heart for his previous meal, that man wasn't worried about the next one. Not only was he taking one day at a time as he faced the seemingly impossible task of starting all over, but he was also taking one hour at a time.

Jesus said, ". . . do not worry about tomorrow" (Matt. 6:34). He doesn't want us to be burdened with the needless weight of anxiety about the future. We have enough to do to deal with the present. We must refuse to fret about things over which we have no control. Then we can rejoice in God's sustaining grace—one day at a time. —R. W. D.

GOD NEVER ASKS US TO BEAR TOMORROW'S
BURDENS WITH TODAY'S GRACE.

Be doers of the Word, and not hearers only.

JAMES 1:22

I read about a man in New York City who died at the age of 63 without ever having had a job. He spent his entire adult life in college. During those years he acquired so many academic degrees that they "looked like the alphabet" behind his name.

Why did this man spend his entire life in college? When he was a child, a wealthy relative died who had named him as a beneficiary in his will. It stated that he was to be given enough money to support him every year as long as he stayed in school. And it was to be discontinued when he had completed his education.

Unfortunately, he spent thousands of hours listening to professors and reading books but never "doing." He acquired more and more knowledge but didn't put it into practice.

This reminds me of what James said: "Be doers of the Word, and not hearers only." Hearing must be matched by doing. —R. W. D.

FIRST WE PORE OVER GOD'S WORD, THEN WE LET HIS LOVE POUR THROUGH US.

Christ also suffered for us, leaving us an example.

1 PETER 2:21

A former missionary told the story of two rugged, powerful mountain goats who met on a narrow pathway joining two mountain ridges. On one side was a chasm 1,000 feet deep; on the other, a steep cliff rising straight up. So narrow was the trail that there was no room to turn around, and the goats could not back up without falling. What would they do? Finally, instead of fighting for the right to pass, one of the goats knelt down and made himself as flat as possible. The other goat then walked over him, and they both proceeded safely.

In a sense, this is what Jesus Christ did for us when He left heaven's glory and came to this earth to die for our sins. He saw us trapped between our sin and God's righteousness with no way to help ourselves. He humbled Himself by giving up His right to use His divine power. He came in the likeness of men and took the form of a servant (Phil. 2:5–8). Then, by dying for sinful mankind, He let us "walk over Him" so that we could experience forgiveness and receive eternal life.
—D. C. E.

CHRIST EMPTIED HIMSELF. BEHOLD OUR PATTERN!

ST. AMBROSE

I will praise the LORD with my whole heart.

PSALM 111:1

The annual golf outing for the men of our church provided a good time of fun and laughter. Slices, hooks, and complete misses provided groans and embarrassment. But whenever someone made a long drive, even the men who usually said very little responded to their partner's success by saying, "Good shot!"

One man kept telling his partner, "Great! Great shot!" Words of praise flowed freely during the whole time, some in loud exclamations, others quietly spoken. But every man knew what it was like to encourage another and to receive praise for an accurate drive or a long putt.

The psalmist gave many reasons to praise the Creator and Provider of all the blessings of life. He mentioned God's great works (Ps. 111:2), His righteousness (v. 3), grace and compassion (v. 4), faithfulness (v. 8), and redemption (v. 9). If we can compliment a good golf shot or some other small accomplishment, shouldn't we compliment God for His great goodness? —D. L. B.

YOU CAN NEVER PRAISE GOD TOO MUCH.

I must work the works of Him who sent Me while it is day.

JOHN 9:4

The advertisement was for Ford cars. It was a cartoon of two men standing on a busy street corner, each holding a large sign in front of him. One man's sign carried this sobering message: "The world will end tomorrow." The other man was standing just around the corner of a building. His sign read: "That still gives you all day today to shop your Ford dealer's year-end clearance."

If we knew that today were our last day on earth, is there anything we would do differently? Maybe no major adjustments in our lifestyle would be necessary. But most of us could probably think of a letter we had intended to write, a visit we had hoped to make, or a broken relationship we were going to try to mend.

Tomorrow may not come, but you still have today to obey. Let's heed what God's Spirit would have us do. —D. J. D.

DELAYED OBEDIENCE IS THE BROTHER OF DISOBEDIENCE.

For all things come from You,
and of Your own we have given You.

1 CHRONICLES 29:14

According to a story I once heard, a little boy followed the church treasurer each Sunday morning as he carried the offering plates out of the auditorium. Then the boy intently watched the man count the offering and put it in the safe. At first the man ignored him, but after several weeks he finally asked, "Son, why do you follow me around every Sunday?" The boy looked up at the treasurer and said, "The preacher says that the offering is for God, and I want to see you give it to Him!"

This story caused me to wonder what it would be like if we could see the Lord and had to place our offerings directly into His hands. Would our motives have to change? Would we give any more than we do now? Would we be more cheerful in our giving? Whether your money goes to support your local church, a missionary, or a Christian ministry, always give with one thought in mind: This is for the Lord! —P. R. V.

WE SHOW OUR LOVE FOR CHRIST BY
WHAT WE DO WITH WHAT WE HAVE.

Hear, my children, the instruction of a father,
and give attention to know understanding.

PROVERBS 4:1

Carl Frost and his family were living in Nigeria during the late 1960s. When electricity became available in their village, each Nigerian family got a single light in their hut. Awed by this technology the people began staying inside in the evenings rather than gathering around the tribal fire.

Author Max De Pree relates how this change had an adverse effect on the heritage of the people: "The light-bulb watching began to replace the customary nighttime gatherings by the tribal fire, where the tribal storytellers, the elders, would pass along the history of the tribe. The tribe was losing its history in the light of a few electric bulbs."

Our children and grandchildren need to snuggle up beside dad or grandpa, or sit on mom's or grandma's lap and hear of the values and experiences of their ancestors. Maybe it's a story of faith in God in the midst of adversity, or a small incident of kindness. Let's take time to share His-tory with young minds whose lives can be shaped for eternity. —D. J. D.

A CHRISTIAN HERITAGE IS THE BEST
LEGACY WE CAN LEAVE OUR CHILDREN.

He who calls you is faithful, who also will do it.

1 THESSALONIANS 5:24

Imagine what the game of bowling would be like if you couldn't see the pins you were trying to hit. In 1933, Bill Knox did just that—and bowled a perfect game.

In Philadelphia's Olney Alleys, Bill had a screen placed just above the foul line to obscure his view of the lane. His purpose was to demonstrate the technique of spot bowling, which involves throwing the ball at a selected floor mark on the near end of the lane. Like many bowlers, Bill knew that you can do better if you aim at a mark close to you that's in line with the pins. He proved his point with a perfect 300 game of 12 strikes in a row.

Spot bowling illustrates part of a wise approach to life. When Paul wrote to the Thessalonians about the return of Christ, he reminded them that the ultimate goal of their salvation was to "be preserved blameless at the coming of our Lord Jesus Christ" (5:23). Paul taught them to focus their eyes on near actions that were in line with that goal. He added that this would be accomplished through the power of Christ (vv. 23–24). —M. R. D. II

WE KEEP ETERNITY'S GOAL IN SIGHT BY WALKING DAILY IN THE LIGHT.

Having begun in the Spirit, are you now
being made perfect by the flesh?

GALATIANS 3:3

Farmer Johnson smiled as he proudly strolled out of the hardware store with a brand-new chainsaw that was guaranteed to cut five big oak trees an hour. Twenty-four hours later, however, his smile was gone. With obvious frustration, Johnson was back at the store complaining that the saw would never cut five trees an hour. "Why, it only cut five trees all day long!" he said.

Somewhat puzzled, the store owner stepped outside with the saw, gave the cord a rip, and fired up the steel-toothed beast. The deafening roar of the saw startled Johnson so badly that he stumbled trying to get away. "What's that noise?" he gasped.

Johnson's mistake in cutting down trees without starting up the chainsaw is similar to our foolishness when we try to follow Christ in our own strength. We get frustrated and spiritually exhausted when we try to make life work on our terms. We cannot live a victorious Christian life by our own strength but by the Spirit of Christ who lives within (Rom. 8:9–11). —M. R. D. II

A WILLING HEART MUST ALWAYS BE KEPT
UNDER THE CONTROL OF A WISE HEAD.

Even the winds and the sea obey Him.

MATTHEW 8:27

Ocean waves can be awesome in size and power. Sailors have measured waves at 60 feet, higher than most houses. In 1933 the Navy tanker Ramapo was hit by a wave 112 feet high! And on a wild, stormy night at Tillamook Rock off the coast of Oregon, a wave picked up a rock that weighed 135 pounds and smashed it into the lighthouse 100 feet above the water line.

Waves on inland lakes can have tremendous power too. The *Edmund Fitzgerald* sank in Lake Superior after being smashed by 30-foot waves.

Sometimes our emotions hit us like the waves of a turbulent sea. One after another, waves of hurt, humiliation, uselessness, isolation, anger, and fear pound us. We're sure we're going under. At those times we need to call on the Lord. He's the one with the authority and power to calm the angry waves within us. He can bring peace to our troubled hearts. —D. C. E.

THE ONE WHO CALMS THE OCEANS CAN CALM OUR FEARFUL HEARTS.

By prayer and supplication . . . let your
requests be made known to God.

PHILIPPIANS 4:6

The story is told of a man who got a permit to open the first tavern in a small town. The members of a local church were strongly opposed to the bar, so they began to pray that God would intervene. A few days before the tavern was scheduled to open, lightning hit the structure and it burned to the ground.

The people of the church were surprised but pleased—until they received notice that the would-be tavern owner was suing them. He contended that their prayers were responsible for the burning of the building. They denied the charge.

At the conclusion of the preliminary hearing, the judge wryly remarked, "At this point I don't know what my decision will be, but it seems that the tavern owner believes in the power of prayer and these church people don't."

Lord, thank You for answering our prayers even when our faith is weak. Increase our faith and help us to pray more expectantly!
—H. V. L.

PRAYER WITHOUT EXPECTANCY MAY BE UNBELIEF IN DISGUISE.

We know . . . we shall be like Him.

1 JOHN 3:2

*A*nother day. Another strip of wallpaper goes up. Another wall gets painted. . . That's the way it's been around our house for the past year or so as we've tackled a major remodeling project. Living in an unfinished house where you have to push paint cans and ladders out of the way to get to the kitchen can be a frustrating experience.

But once in a while we can visualize the finished product as we peer through the drywall dust. We have hope; we know that one day we will be able to live in our house the way people are supposed to—with carpet on the floors and the tools put away.

Hope. Completion. Those two words are even more meaningful to Christians. Our lives always seem to be in a state of remodeling. We are often frustrated by our inability to be complete in our likeness to Christ. But just as our family keeps painting and papering because we know the finished product will be worth it, so also we as believers can keep going because we have the sure hope that someday we will be like the Lord Jesus (1 John 3:2). —J. D. B.

GOD FORMED US; CHRIST TRANSFORMS US.

Remember that Jesus Christ . . . was raised from the dead.

2 TIMOTHY 2:8

Franciszek Gajowniczek was a Nazi prisoner in Auschwitz when a fellow inmate escaped. The standard discipline when anyone escaped was to select 10 men at random and place them in a cell where they were left to starve to death. When Gajowniczek heard his name read, he sobbed, "My wife and my children." At that moment a Franciscan priest and fellow inmate named Kolbe stepped forward and said, "I will die in his place. I have no wife or children." The Commandant granted his request.

Since that time Gajowniczek has gone back every year to Auschwitz on August 14 to remember the man who died for him on that date in 1941. And in his yard he has placed a plaque to honor this priest and to remind others of his great sacrifice.

About A.D. 68, Paul wrote his young pastor friend Timothy from a prison, reminding him that the Savior's death and resurrection provided hope, confidence, and the prospect of glory (2 Tim. 2:8–13). Then he told him to remind others of these wonderful truths (v. 14).
—H. V. L.

**OTHERS WILL KNOW WHAT CHRIST CAN DO,
WHEN YOU TELL WHAT HE HAS DONE FOR YOU.**

*God . . . comforts us . . . that we may be
able to comfort those who are in any trouble.*

2 CORINTHIANS 1:3–4

A mother who lost her son asked an elderly Chinese philosopher how to overcome her deep grief. "I can help you, but you must first bring me some mustard seed," said the old wise man. "But you must get it at a home where there has never been any loss or sorrow."

Eagerly the woman started her search, but in every home she visited was someone who had lost a loved one or had known some heartbreaking loss. Returning without any mustard seed, she exclaimed, "How selfish I have been! Sorrow is common to all." "Ah," said the philosopher, "you have learned a valuable lesson. Because you know sorrow, you can sympathize with others and comfort them. And when you do, your own sorrow will be lessened."

The best comforters are those whom God has comforted and who are willing to comfort others. —H. G. B.

GOD COMFORTS US TO MAKE US COMFORTERS.

The LORD shall preserve your going out
and your coming in . . . forevermore.

PSALM 121:8

One of my friends who had looked forward to receiving a substantial monthly benefit at retirement is now without a job. The company he worked for went bankrupt. Moreover, the retirement funds no longer exist. Suddenly the future for him and his wife is far less secure than he thought.

Another friend, a man with financial security who had anticipated a decade or more of happy retirement, is terminally ill. The good years he was anticipating are not going to become a reality.

As I reflect upon these two people, I realize that in this world we have no absolute security about either our finances or our health. Our only complete security is in God. —H. V. L.

OUR GREATEST NEED CAN NEVER EXCEED
OUR GREATEST RESOURCE—GOD.

I have no greater joy than to hear that my children walk in truth.

3 JOHN 4

The truth of God is a wonderful asset to a Christian. Joni Tada likened the value of God's truth to an experience in her childhood. She wrote, "At four, I was too young to have my own horse, and I'm not sure a horse fit for a four-year-old could have kept up with my father and sisters. So when we went horseback riding, I sat behind my father on his big horse. With my tiny hands, I'd hang on to the back of his belt and away we'd go. I'd bounce up and down in the saddle, sliding this way and that, but as long as I had a strong hold on that belt, I knew I was safe."

God's truth is like that belt. It's strong and reassuring, and we can hold on to it amid the turns and bumps of life. He is our all-loving, all-powerful God, and He does not change. He will give us all the help we need. —D. C. E.

**IF WE HOLD ON TO GOD'S TRUTH,
WE WON'T BE TRAPPED BY SATAN'S LIES.**

A soft answer turns away wrath, but a harsh word stirs up anger.

PROVERBS 15:1

In 1952, President Harry Truman appointed Newbold Morris to a very important post. His duty was to keep a close check on crime and mismanagement in government affairs.

On one occasion, however, Morris was called before a Senate sub-committee to answer questions about the sale of some ships by his own company in New York. The interrogation became intense and emotions ran high.

Then Morris remembered a note his wife had given him that morning. Sensing the need to calm everyone down, he called out above the clamor, "Wait a minute. I have a note here from my wife." Pulling it out of his pocket, he read the words, "Keep your shirt on." There was a burst of laughter and the tension was eased.

Whenever we are in a tension-filled situation, either with just one individual or in a group, we need to remember that "a soft answer turns away wrath." —R. W. D.

STAYING CALM IS THE BEST WAY TO TAKE THE WIND OUT OF AN ANGRY PERSON'S SAILS.

Our citizenship is in heaven.

PHILIPPIANS 3:20

One of the terms used often during the 1992 Summer Olympics by television sports commentators was *dual citizenship*.

One athlete with dual citizenship was a swimmer named Martin Zubero. He was born in the United States, where he has lived nearly all of his life. He attended the University of Florida and trained for competition in the U.S. However, he was swimming under the colors of Spain. Why? His father is a citizen of Spain and so Martin is too. At the Olympics, he chose to represent his father's nation, to which he felt greater allegiance.

Christians too have dual citizenship. We are citizens of this world, no matter what nation we live in, and as followers of Christ we are also citizens of heaven (Phil. 3:20). We have all the rights and privileges that accompany being a child of God. He is not only our heavenly Father but our King, and our first loyalty must be to His kingdom. —D. C. E.

WE LIVE IN THIS WORLD, BUT OUR ALLEGIANCE IS TO HEAVEN.

Put on tender mercies, kindness, humility, meekness, longsuffering.

COLOSSIANS 3:12

Ken Robinson, who is now a pastor, at one time served as a police officer. He said people treated him differently when he was in uniform than when he was off duty and wearing plain clothes. Something about the badge and "blues" gained him instant respect and authority.

He was often addressed as "Sir." When he told people something, they believed him. And when he gave an order, they were quick to obey. Robinson concluded, "I guess the clothes made the difference. And in uniform, I acted with more confidence."

In Colossians 3, the apostle Paul told followers of Christ to put on a new uniform. First he described the clothes we are to "put off" (vv. 8–9). Then he told us what kind of uniform we are to "put on" (vv. 12–14). In place of anger, wrath, slander, dirty language, and lies, we are to put on mercy, kindness, humility, gentleness, patience, forgiveness, and love.

What you "wear" makes a big difference. —D. C. E.

MAY I LIVE SO ALL CAN SEE THE LOVE OF CHRIST REVEALED IN ME.

Be kind to one another, tenderhearted, forgiving one another.

EPHESIANS 4:32

A young factory worker noticed one day that a valuable tool was missing from his toolbox. Later he recognized it in the toolbox of a fellow employee.

The young man was the only Christian in the shop, and he wanted to have a good testimony for Christ. So he went to the man and said, "I see you have one of my tools, but you may keep it if you need it." Then he went on with his work and put the incident out of his mind.

During the next two weeks, the person who had taken the tool tried to soothe his conscience. First he offered the young man something of equal value, then he offered to help him on some home projects, and finally he slipped some money into his coat pocket. Eventually, the co-workers became good friends, and the one-time tool thief admitted he couldn't resist the man's kindness.

Kindness is probably the most effective tool Christians have in their kit of virtues. Oh, for grace to extend love to others, even as God for Christ's sake has loved us! —H. G. B.

NEED TO REPAIR A RELATIONSHIP? TRY KINDNESS.

Your testimonies also are my delight and my counselors.

PSALM 119:24

Several years ago, these words appeared on the cover of the Grand Rapids telephone directory: "Look in the book first." It was a reminder to check its pages for numbers before calling the operator.

That reminded me of a spiritual parallel: Before we meet any challenge or seek the Lord's blessing on our lives, we should look first in His Book for His direction and guidance. When we neglect to look in the Bible, we risk getting involved in relationships that He cannot bless and in activities that God does not approve.

In his book *Hints to Young Christians,* O. T. Gifford made the following comment: "If you're getting lazy, read James. If your faith is below par, read Paul. If you're impatient, consider the book of Job. If you're a little strong-headed, go and see Moses. If you're weak-kneed, have a look at Elijah. If there is no song in your heart, listen to David."

—H. G. B.

LOOK IN THE BOOK.

I will praise You, for I am fearfully and wonderfully made.

PSALM 139:14

In the late 1970s, biophysicist Harold J. Morowitz of Yale University reached some startling conclusions about what it would cost to make a human body. Taking into consideration the proteins, enzymes, RNA, DNA, amino acids, and other complex biochemicals that make up the stuff of life, Dr. Morowitz states, "Fashioning this chemical shopping list into human cells might cost six quadrillion dollars. Assembling the resulting heap of cells into tissue, the tissue into organs, and the organs into a warm body might drain all the treasuries of the world, with no guarantee of success."

As we think about this, we are astounded at the wisdom and creative power of the Lord who made us. But we're even more than a physical body. God has also given each of us an eternal soul that is worth more than the whole world (Matt. 16:26). We stand in awe at His marvelous creation! —R. W. D.

THE LORD WHO GAVE YOU LIFE WANTS
TO BE THE CENTER OF YOUR LIFE.

The father shall make known Your truth to the children.

Isaiah 38:19

*I*t's time for the lazy days of summer to give way to the busy days of fall. Time again for school to start. Getting youngsters ready for school can leave parents gasping for breath.

But there's more to getting the children ready than filling their backpack and getting them to the bus on time. They must also be prepared spiritually. Before they hit the books, they need to know that the most important things they will ever learn come from the Book: the Bible.

There are many ways this can be done. One family takes time before school to have Bible reading. While Dad and the kids eat, Mom reads a chapter as they work through the whole Bible. Another family uses the time to read and discuss shorter passages—Dad taking one child, Mom the other. Some parents use the night before to share scriptural truths.

Before anyone else has a chance to educate our children, we need to teach them about God. —J. D. B.

IF CHILDREN ARE TO FIND THEIR WAY TO GOD, SOMEONE MUST POINT THE WAY.

The LORD gives wisdom; from His mouth
come knowledge and understanding.

PROVERBS 2:6

An investment company's full-page ad in the *Wall Street Journal* began with these words: "Information is everywhere. Insight is all too rare. For insight goes beyond information to discern underlying truths."

Today, we are long on information and short on insight. Television offers scores of channels. Encyclopedias and world atlases are on compact disks (CDs). Online databases give us the temperature in Hong Kong and the baseball score in Birmingham. We're wired and tired from trying to grasp the meaning of all we know.

Years ago, a friend encouraged me to read a chapter from Proverbs each day. One chapter each day takes me through this marvelous book of God's wisdom every month. "You can get knowledge in college," my friend said, "but wisdom comes from God."

One chapter of Proverbs every day. Try it next month and see how God's Word will give you the wisdom to transform information into insight. —D. C. M.

YOU CAN GET KNOWLEDGE IN COLLEGE,
BUT WISDOM COMES FROM GOD.

Fulfill my joy by being like-minded, . . . being of one accord.

PHILIPPIANS 2:2

Long lines of cars were filling up the huge parking lot of a church where I was attending a conference. As I parked, I noticed the word *Love* on a lightpost in one section. In another area, I saw the word *Faithfulness.* The next day I pulled into a different lot at the same church and saw *Patience* on another sign. Like numbers in a mall parking lot, these words help people find their cars.

No doubt these signs served another purpose. After each session, some people were in a hurry to get home—even cutting others off to get out of the lot. Patience wore thin and tempers flared. *How appropriate those signs are! I* thought. It's amazing how quickly the love we have for our brothers and sisters in Christ can disappear in a parking lot!

The testing of our faith may come through heavy burdens, but it's just as likely to occur in a checkout line, on the expressway, or in a parking lot. —D. C. E.

THE CLEAR SIGN OF YOUR FAITH IS NOT WHAT YOU SAY BUT WHAT YOU DO.

Jesus . . . said, "It is finished!"

JOHN 19:30

*O*utside Madrid stands an ancient monastery where the kings of Spain have been buried. The architect designed an elongated arch so flat that the reigning monarch insisted it could not hold the structure above it.

Against the architect's protest, the king ordered that a column be placed underneath the arch as a safety precaution. After the king died, the architect revealed that he had deliberately made the column a quarter of an inch too short—and the arch had never sagged!

Nothing need be, or can be, added to the finished work of Christ on Calvary to sustain the weight of the world's salvation. With utter assurance, then, we can rest our eternal hope on that one all-important word, "Finished!" —V. C. G.

WE ARE SAVED NOT BY WHAT WE DO BUT BY WHAT CHRIST HAS DONE.

*We are . . . pleased rather to be absent from
the body and to be present with the Lord.*

2 CORINTHIANS 5:8

The young musicians hired to play for the Duke of Austria's summer festivities were ready to go home. Summer was over and they were tired, but the Duke kept them there.

The brilliant classical composer Franz Joseph Haydn was sympathetic and offered to help them. So he composed a unique symphony that began with full orchestra. As the symphony progressed, fewer instruments were included in the score. One by one, as their parts were finished, the musicians took their instruments and walked off the stage.

By the end of the composition, only two musicians remained— the first and second violinists playing a beautiful duet. The Duke got the point. Shortly afterward, he sent the grateful musicians home. To this day *Haydn's Symphony No. 45* is known as "The Farewell Symphony."

God's people are part of another farewell symphony. One by one, God is calling His people home. And one day the trumpet of God will sound for all who believe on Him. What a day of rejoicing that will be!—D. C. E.

AT DEATH, GOD'S PEOPLE DON'T SAY "GOODBYE" BUT "SEE YOU LATER."

We . . . declare to you that eternal life which
was with the Father and was manifested to us.

1 JOHN 1:2

When Apollo 11 neared the moon in July 1969, the editors of *The New York Times* felt their coverage of the first step on lunar soil should go beyond headlines and photos to embrace an achievement shared by all humanity. So they asked Pulitzer Prize-winner Archibald MacLeish to write a poem. The day after Neil Armstrong and Edwin Aldrin Jr. walked on the moon, the front page contained these words: *You were a wonder to us, . . . a light beyond our light, our lives—perhaps a meaning to us . . . our hands have touched you in your depth of night.*

That day, through the hands of others, we touched the moon.

The apostle John wrote some memorable words about an even more significant historical event—the visit of God's Son to this planet. He wrote, "That which was from the beginning, . . .which we have looked upon, and our hands have handled" (1 John 1:1, 3). As surely as John held Him in the flesh, we can grasp the Son of God through faith. —D. C. M.

WE CAN COME TO JESUS BECAUSE JESUS CAME TO US.

You were . . . redeemed . . . with the precious blood of Christ.

1 PETER 1:18–19

All America waited anxiously. Many of us prayed. Captain Scott O'Grady's F-16 had been shot down as he was flying over Serbia. Had he been killed or captured? Was he seriously injured? The hours ticked by. Five days passed. On the sixth day another pilot picked up a faint message from O'Grady's radio. He was alive, managing somehow to hide from hostile soldiers.

Immediately all the resources needed for a daring rescue operation were set in motion. O'Grady was snatched up to safety by a helicopter—and the US rejoiced. Newsweek magazine reported that the weapons and machinery used for the rescue of that one pilot were valued at $6 billion.

We can't estimate the value of one human soul—because we could never calculate the price God paid to rescue us. He sent His Son to become our Savior. Jesus Christ died on the cross and shed His precious blood to rescue us from the kingdom of darkness (1 Pet. 1:18–19). If all the stars in all the galaxies were changed into platinum, that incalculable sum could not begin to purchase our salvation! —V. C. G.

JESUS GAVE HIS ALL FOR ME—HOW CAN I GIVE HIM LESS?

*I call to remembrance the genuine faith that is
in you, which dwelt first in your grandmother.*

2 TIMOTHY 1:5

When a team of Christians visited Stavropol, Russia, in 1994 to hand out Bibles, a local citizen said he recalled seeing Bibles in an old warehouse. They had been confiscated in the 1930s when Stalin was sending believers to the gulags. Amazingly, the Bibles were still there.

Among those who showed up to load them into trucks was a young agnostic student just wanting to earn a day's wage. But soon he slipped away from the job to steal a Bible. A team member went looking for him and found him sitting in a corner weeping. Out of the hundreds of Bibles, he had picked up one that bore the handwritten signature of his own grandmother. Persecuted for her faith, she had no doubt prayed often for her family and her city. God used that grandmother's Bible to convict that young man.

Paul encouraged Timothy by recalling the faith of his grandmother and mother. Although Timothy's faith was his own, it was deeply linked to theirs. What an admonition to us who are parents and grandparents to be faithful! —D. J. D.

**BETTER THAN HAVING CHILDREN BEAR YOUR NAME
IS TO HAVE THEM BEAR CHRIST'S NAME.**

Whoever loses his life for My sake will find it.

MATTHEW 16:25

A man who habitually slept as long as he could every morning, awoke one day even later than usual. Looking at the clock, he bolted out of bed, threw on some clothes, splashed cold water on his face, quickly combed his hair, gulped down a glass of milk, grabbed his briefcase, gave his wife a kiss as he ran out the door, and raced to catch the bus. He barely got on it as it began to pull away. Dropping a coin in the meter, he lurched down the aisle toward a seat. Suddenly he looked around and breathlessly blurted out, "Where's this bus going anyway?"

This story reminds me of many people today. Taken up with the rush of everyday activities, they neglect to make sure they're headed in the right direction.

If we surrender our lives to God, and let Him take the controls (Matt. 16:24), we'll be on the road of joy in this life and will have eternal reward in the life to come (v. 28). —R. W. D.

**MANY PEOPLE ARE MAKING GOOD TIME,
BUT THEY'RE GOING THE WRONG WAY.**

You meant evil against me; but God meant it for good.

GENESIS 50:20

The book *In His Steps* may have earned less money for its author than any other bestseller in history. Charles M. Sheldon wrote it in 1896, and it was first published by a religious weekly magazine. The magazine's publisher failed to meet copyright regulations, so Sheldon lost legal ownership of the book. Scores of publishers then sold millions of copies, and the author couldn't claim any royalties.

Forty years after Charles Sheldon "lost" his book, he said, "I am very thankful that owing to the defective copyright, the book has had a larger reading on account of the great number of publishers."

Joseph too experienced losses. He was sold into slavery by his brothers (Gen. 37:20–27). Then he lost his position in Potiphar's household because of a false accusation (Gen. 39:1–20). And yet he did not blame anyone. Instead he recognized that God had orchestrated the events of his life for the eventual good of others. —D. C. M.

**WHAT APPEARS TO BE HUMAN TRAGEDY IS
OFTEN THE SEED OF DIVINE TRIUMPH.**

Let your "Yes" be "Yes," and your "No," "No."

MATTHEW 5:37

Shortly before his death, the Duke of Burgundy was presiding over the Cabinet Council of France. A proposal was made that would violate an existing treaty but would secure important advantages for the country. Many "good" reasons were offered to justify this action. The Duke listened in silence. When all had spoken, he closed the conference without giving approval. Placing his hand on a copy of the original agreement, he said with firmness in his voice, "Gentlemen, we have a treaty!"

It's a strong temptation these days to abandon our word in favor of personal advantage or financial gain. As believers in Christ, however, our responsibility is to remain true to our word so that our Lord is glorified.

So, when you give your word, keep it! "Let your 'Yes' be 'Yes,' and your 'No,' 'No.'" —R. W. D.

WHEN YOU GIVE YOUR WORD, KEEP IT.

Oh, the depth of the riches both of
the wisdom and knowledge of God!

ROMANS 11:33

While learning to use a new computer, I was troubled by a faint clicking sound that indicated it was working even though nothing was happening on the screen. The manufacturer's representative on the help hotline said, "No problem. The computer is probably running an application you can't see and is working in the background."

As I thought about the phrase "working in the background," I began to realize how visually oriented I am in my relationship with God. If I can't see something, I assume it's not happening. But that's not the way God operates.

Is there a situation in your life today where you cannot see God working? Perhaps someone you love is obstinately refusing to respond to God. Even though it may appear that nothing is happening, God is at work—behind the scenes, in the background, accomplishing His purpose. —D. C. M.

**IN THE DRAMA OF LIFE, GOD IS THE
DIRECTOR BEHIND THE SCENES.**

*In everything by prayer and supplication, with thanksgiving,
let your requests be made known to God.*

PHILIPPIANS 4:6

Author A. B. Simpson told about an old farmer who plowed around a large rock in his field year after year. He had broken one cultivator and two plowshares by hitting it. Each time he saw that obstacle, he grumbled about how much trouble the rock had caused.

One day he decided to dig it up and be done with it. Putting a large crowbar under one side, he found to his surprise that the rock was less than a foot thick. Soon he had pried it out of the ground and was carting it away in his wagon. He smiled to think how that "big" old rock had caused him so much needless frustration.

Not every trouble can be removed as easily as that stone. But prayer is an effective way to handle difficulties of all sizes. Using the leverage of prayer with our problems can keep us from becoming victims of worry. —D. J. D.

FERVENT PRAYER DISPELS ANXIOUS CARE.

*The manifestation of the Spirit is given
to each one for the profit of all.*

1 CORINTHIANS 12:7

A well-known coach was once asked, "How much does college football contribute to the national physical-fitness picture?"

"Nothing," the coach replied abruptly.

"Why not?" the startled interviewer asked.

"Well," said the coach, "the way I see it, you have 22 men down on the field desperately needing a rest and 40,000 people in the stands desperately needing some exercise."

A similar situation exists in many churches today. When you compare the members who merely attend with those who actively participate, you often find a rather pathetic situation. It's not unusual to have a small group of diligent Christian workers struggling "down on the field" while others in the congregation act like spectators.

My friend, if you've been sitting in the stands, you're badly needed down on the field! —M. R. D. II

CHRISTIANS SHOULD BE ON THE FRONTLINES, NOT THE SIDELINES.

I have learned in whatever state I am, to be content.

PHILIPPIANS 4:11

During 1997 as the world focused on the deaths of Princess Diana and Mother Teresa, another significant passing went almost unnoticed. Austrian psychiatrist Viktor Frankl died on September 2 at the age of 93.

During World War II, Dr. Frankl was imprisoned at Auschwitz, where he was stripped of his identity as a medical doctor and forced to work as a common laborer. His father, mother, brother, and wife died in the concentration camps. All his notes, which represented his life's work, were destroyed. Yet Frankl emerged from Auschwitz believing that "everything can be taken from a man but one thing: the last of the human freedoms—to choose one's attitude in any given set of circumstances."

We may not be able to choose our circumstances, but we can choose our attitude toward them. Whatever our circumstances may be, we can draw on the power of Christ for the strength to face them. —D. C. M.

A GOOD ATTITUDE—IT'S YOUR CHOICE.

Let your eyes look straight ahead.

PROVERBS 4:25

I had always heard that if a farmer keeps his eyes on a distant object while he's plowing, he'll make a straight furrow. So I tested the principle when I mowed my lawn. Sure enough, my first cut was a straight swath of new-mown turf.

If you can plow a straight furrow or mow in a straight line by keeping your eyes fixed on a distant object, surely the principle should also be true of life—especially if the object on which you fix your gaze is the same yesterday, today, and forever.

According to Proverbs, the wise person can walk the straight path and not be diverted. In fact, the whole book of Proverbs is about following a straight path. But the Bible doesn't just advise, "Be wise!" It introduces us to Jesus Christ. The truly important question is our relationship to Him. —D. J. D.

OUR WISDOM IS FOLLY UNLESS WE'RE FOLLOWING CHRIST.

Go over this Jordan, you and all this people.

JOSHUA 1:2

Modern society emphasizes efficiency and convenience but minimizes interaction among people. For example, a person using the phone may hear recorded messages: "For account information, press 1." "At the tone, leave a message." "For flight information, press 2."

Although we may think life would be easier if we didn't have to deal with troublesome, time-consuming relationships, God calls us to operate from a different perspective. As followers of Christ, we are to remain in the people business.

When Joshua succeeded Moses as the leader of Israel, God commanded him, "Arise, go over this Jordan, you and all this people, to the land which I am giving you" (Josh. 1:2). I might have questioned the Lord, "This group has a terrible track record. Wouldn't it be easier to leave the complainers and second-guessers behind? Isn't it my job to conquer the land?" But the Lord had said, "You and *all* this people." —D. C. M.

PEOPLE ARE AT THE HEART OF GOD'S HEART.

Let us not love in word or in
tongue, but in deed and in truth.

1 JOHN 3:18

A young woman backpacking in Colorado encountered another woman hobbling down a mountain trail. On one foot she wore an improvised shoe made of green twigs wrapped with a strip of cloth.

"Lost one boot crossing a stream," she explained. "Hope I can get down the mountain before dark."

The first hiker reached into her own pack and took out a sport sandal. "Wear this," she said. "You can mail it to me when you get home."

The woman gratefully accepted the sandal and set off down the trail. A few days later the sandal arrived in the mail with a note saying: "I passed several people who noticed my predicament, but you're the only one who offered any help. It made all the difference. Thanks for sharing your sandal with me."

The Bible says love can be seen and touched—it's tangible. Real love takes action. —D. C. M.

YOU MAY GIVE WITHOUT LOVING,
BUT YOU CAN'T LOVE WITHOUT GIVING.

The eternal God is your refuge, and
underneath are the everlasting arms.

DEUTERONOMY 33:27

tty Hillesum was a young Jewish woman living in
Amsterdam in 1942. During that time, the Nazis were
arresting Jews and herding them off to concentration camps. As she
awaited inevitable arrest, and with a fear of the unknown, she began
to read the Bible—and met Jesus. She simply put her hand in God's
hand and found rare courage and confidence.

Etty wrote in her diary: "Soon the ring will be closed and no
one at all will be able to come to our aid. But I don't feel that I am in
anybody's clutches. I feel safe in God's arms. And whether I am sitting
at my beloved old desk in the Jewish district or in a labor camp under
SS guards, I shall feel safe in God's arms." —V. C. G.

YOU CAN BE CONFIDENT ABOUT TOMORROW
IF YOU WALK WITH GOD TODAY.

Your heavenly Father knows that you need all these things.

MATTHEW 6:32

While waiting for a tire to be repaired, I began talking with a man who farmed nearby. "Sure need rain," he said. "Don't know what we're gonna do if it doesn't rain."

"A lot different from last year," I said.

"A year ago it was so wet I couldn't get in the field," the man replied. Then he paused and said, "You know, I've been farming around here for 41 years and it's always the same—either too wet or too dry. I don't know why I bother to talk about it in the first place!"

We laughed together and I went on my way, pondering what he had said and its relation to all the things I was worried about that day.

For every essential element in our lives today, God would be pleased to have us trade worry for trust and say, "Thank You, kind heavenly Father. You already know what I need. So I'll trust You to take care of me." —D. C. M.

THE WAY TO BE ANXIOUS ABOUT NOTHING IS TO BE PRAYERFUL ABOUT EVERYTHING.

"You shall be My witnesses . . . to the end of the earth."

ACTS 1:8

*M*issionary Keith Gustafson was forced to leave the Congo because of the civil war that erupted in 1997. He reported that as the fighting spread, people in the remote area where he lived knew that soldiers were approaching because of the message of the drums. Down the trails and along the riverbanks came the chilling drumbeat that warned of danger.

The drums of the Congo are also used to alert the tribes when there's been a death, to announce a birth, or to call a meeting. They serve as a general news alert; a messenger follows up with additional information.

We have the opportunity to deliver a news alert to the people with whom we come in contact every day. Our manner of speech and our moral standards can help prepare the way to share the gospel. We can follow up our general testimony with the specific message of the gospel. —D. C. E.

THEY WITNESS BEST WHO WITNESS WITH THEIR LIVES AND THEIR LIPS.

I know whom I have believed and am persuaded that
He is able to keep what I have committed to Him.

2 TIMOTHY 1:12

A crowd gazed in awe as a tightrope walker inched his way across Niagara Falls. The people cheered when he accomplished the feat.

Then he turned to a man and said, "Do you think I could carry someone across?" "Sure," the man replied.

"Let's go then!" "No thanks!" the man exclaimed. So the tightrope walker asked another man, "What about you? Will you trust me?" "Yes, I will," he said. That man climbed onto his shoulders, and with the water roaring below they reached the other side.

Hidden in this story is a spiritual challenge each of us must face. Our sinfulness is a yawning chasm between us and God, and we are unable to cross it. Only Jesus is able to bring us safely to the other side. But we must repent and trust Him with our lives. —J. E. Y.

CHRIST IS THE BRIDGE OVER THE CHASM OF SIN.

*The natural man does not receive the things of
the Spirit of God, for they are foolishness to him.*

1 CORINTHIANS 2:14

Switzerland is known for its scenic mountains and beautiful waterfalls. A visitor to that picturesque country observed: "Some guidebooks name the time when rainbows may be seen on many of the waterfalls in Switzerland. One day, when I was at Lauterbrunnen, I went to the famous Staubbach Falls and watched and waited. Others did the same, and we all went away quite disappointed. The next day one of my friends said he would show us how to find the rainbow. So I went again and saw a lovely one, and stood almost in the center of it. Then I found that not only were sunshine and spray necessary to produce a rainbow, but also that it could be seen and enjoyed only at a certain point."

The same is true in the spiritual realm. A person who knows Jesus as Savior is "in Christ," and from that vantage point he can see Jesus as He really is. The Holy Spirit lives in believers and enables them to appreciate and understand the treasures of the Bible. But those who have not received Christ as their Savior remain blind to eternal truths (1 Cor. 2:14). They can see the waterfall—but not the rainbow. —R. W. D.

**WITHOUT THE LIGHT OF GOD'S SPIRIT,
WE'LL BE IN THE DARK ABOUT GOD'S WORD.**

*What will it profit a man if he gains
the whole world, and loses his own soul?*

MARK 8:36

When the great ocean liner Titanic sank in 1912, it
was rumored to have gone down with a fortune in jewels
and gold. That longstanding myth was dispelled, however, by the
discovery of the ship's manifest, which showed that the ship was
carrying raw feathers, linen, straw, hatter's fur, tissue, auto parts,
leather, rabbit hair, elastics, hair nets, and refrigerating equipment.

There is another persistent rumor about riches. It is widely
believed that a wealthy person should be honored and valued,
even though he may be ungodly. On the other hand, a godly, self-
disciplined person is considered by some to be of little worth if he
is not wealthy.

David, the author of Psalm 37, cautioned the poor and needy
not to be envious of the rich and prosperous. This life is only the
beginning of an everlasting existence. So don't look longingly at the
ungodly and their riches. They have no lasting treasures. Instead, wait
with patience for your eternal reward. —M. R. D. II

IT'S BETTER TO BE POOR AND WALK BY FAITH
THAN TO BE RICH AND WALK BY SIGHT.

Your hand shall lead me, and Your right hand shall hold me.

PSALM 139:10

My wife and I love to travel roads we've never been on before. Last fall we drove down a county road in northern Wisconsin. The autumn colors were near their peak, and every turn brought us a thrilling new sight. Maples of red and orange, green pines, and yellow softwoods painted the ever-changing landscape. Not knowing what to expect next made the journey memorable.

One of the many exciting aspects of walking with Christ is that we don't know what's going to happen next. At times we may be uncomfortable with the twists and turns, but God reserves the right to lead us wherever He wants.

As we prayerfully consider what God wants us to do, we can be confident that He will lead us day by day through His Word and by His Spirit within us (Ps. 139:10). We can trust Him with our lives in this great adventure called life. —D. C. E.

YOU DON'T NEED TO SEE THE WAY IF YOU FOLLOW THE ONE WHO IS THE WAY.

The Word of our God stands forever.

ISAIAH 40:8

*S*ecrecy, lawsuits, and technological advances are part of a news item some have called "the greatest achievement of the past 1,000 years." This isn't a recent story of spy satellites or computer programs. It's the story behind Johannes Gutenberg's first-ever printing press—in 1455!

Gutenberg had tried to keep his invention top secret until it was completed, but a lawsuit by heirs of one of his investors revealed what he was working on. His press was a technological marvel that would make possible the mass printing of literature.

When Gutenberg finished his press, the first book he printed was the Bible. That single event would eventually make the Bible by far the most widely distributed book in the world!

Why has this one book attracted so much attention? Why was it Gutenberg's first choice? And why are millions still printed every year? It's simple—the Bible is a supernatural book, the written revelation of God to man. God inspired it, and He preserves it. —J. D. B.

MANY BOOKS CAN INFORM, BUT ONLY THE BIBLE CAN TRANSFORM.

A wholesome tongue is a tree of life.

PROVERBS 15:4

A newspaper obituary caught my eye with this statement: "Services for affable fix-it man are today." Instead of focusing on one of the movers and shakers of society, the article told the story of a seventy-nine-year-old appliance repairman who was known for his integrity, character, and unquenchable happiness.

The president of the company for which the man had worked said, "Half of his job was to go to people's houses and fix the appliances, and the other half was to fix the people. We had a lot of people with problems who requested him by name. He was very jovial, very friendly, and always had a kind word."

No matter what our job, perhaps the most important work we do is helping and encouraging people, especially by what we say.
—D. C. M.

KIND WORDS ARE ALWAYS THE RIGHT KIND.

The LORD is near to all who call upon Him.

PSALM 145:18

*W*hen I was 7 years old, my grandfather was caretaker of a wooded estate. One fall evening I took my toy gun, called for my dog Pal, and headed down a path into the forest. I walked bravely into the woods. Soon, though, it began to get dark and I panicked. "Grandpa!" I shouted.

"I'm right here," he said calmly, only a few yards away. He had seen me go into the woods and had followed me to make sure I was okay. Talk about being relieved!

As followers of Christ, we sometimes venture into unfamiliar territory. We try new things. We take on responsibilities in the work of the Lord that are bigger than we've ever attempted before. It can get pretty scary.

But wherever we go, God is there. His pledge to be near is backed up by His omnipresence. His promise to help us is backed up by His mighty power. He will hear the cries of those who fear Him (Ps. 145:20). —D. C. E.

DARK FEARS FLEE IN THE LIGHT OF GOD'S PRESENCE.

He who does these things shall never be moved.

PSALM 15:5

Recently the city of Hong Kong was blanketed with posters showing a single drop of water splashing into a pool. Each poster bore the words "Hong Kong Against Corruption." The message was clear—integrity or dishonesty permeates a city one person at a time.

It's easy to compromise in little things because they seem to make no difference in society at large. We think, "Why shouldn't I alter the truth, pad my expense reports, or use my employer's time for personal projects when everyone else is doing it? I'm just one drop in the bucket!" Exactly. And every drop helps determine the contents.

What would it mean to our families, our neighborhoods, our cities if you and I lived with integrity according to God's guidelines? Let's do it! Every drop counts. —D. C. M.

INTEGRITY IS CHRISTLIKE CHARACTER IN WORKCLOTHES.

Bring [your children] up in the
training and admonition of the Lord.

EPHESIANS 6:4

Learning a trade as an apprentice is not as involved now as it was in days gone by. Today, when someone is assigned to a department or an individual to learn a job or craft, he does so by observation, instruction, and practice.

But in years past, an apprenticeship often began while the learner was still a young person. He moved right in with his teacher and lived as he lived. He was with the master carpenter or blacksmith 24 hours a day, watching his every move and following his harsh instruction. He learned the skill, but he learned much more than a profession. He was being taught a whole way of life.

This total-life concept is built into the word translated "training" in Ephesians 6:4. It means much more than teaching the Bible and Christian belief, though those are involved. The expectation is that through word and personal example parents will nurture their children and teach them what it means to live for Christ in a practical, daily sense. —D. C. E.

TRAIN UP A CHILD IN THE WAY HE SHOULD GO,
BUT BE SURE YOU GO THAT WAY YOURSELF.

The race is not to the swift, nor the battle to the strong.

ECCLESIASTES 9:11

The newspaper headline read, "Jockey Beats Horse Over Finish Line." The jockey beat the pack by 20 lengths and his horse by one length when he was catapulted out of the saddle and over the finish line. His horse, who had tripped, followed soon after. But the victory went to the second-place finisher named Slip Up. A race official said that the jockey "was so far in front that only a freak accident would stop him, . . . and that's what happened."

Life is filled with unpredictable experiences and events. They seem like stones dropped into the gears of human ingenuity. A strong, healthy man drops dead. A rising young athlete contracts a crippling disease. A person of means suddenly loses everything.

The author of Ecclesiastes reflected on the fact that man is not the master of his destiny, as he so often thinks he is. What can we learn from this? Not to trust our own strength, wisdom, or skill, but to depend on the Lord who alone knows the end from the beginning.
—M. R. D. II

LIVING WITHOUT FAITH IN GOD IS LIKE DRIVING IN THE FOG.

We . . . , beholding as in a mirror the glory of
the Lord, are being transformed into the same image.

2 CORINTHIANS 3:18

Years ago, Walter A. Maier, an eloquent radio preacher, told about an African tribal chief who was presented with a mirror by a visitor. He peered curiously into the glass and commented on the ugliness of the person he saw. When he realized he was looking at himself, he became enraged and smashed the mirror on a rock.

The apostle James described God's Word as a mirror in which we can see ourselves reflected (1:23–24). It shows us that although we were created to reflect God's character, in our fallen condition we are spiritually ugly and marred by sin.

But when we put our faith in Jesus Christ, we are spiritually reborn (John 3:3–8). Then, as we look into God's Word, we see ourselves as God sees us—our ugliness has been transformed into the beauty of Christ's likeness. And we grow in His likeness from that point on. —V. C. G.

THE WORD OF GOD IS THE ONLY MIRROR
THAT CAN TRANSFORM OUR APPEARANCE.

Be strong in the grace that is in Christ Jesus.

2 TIMOTHY 2:1

The story is told about an elderly man who retired after many years in the British Army. One day a man who knew about his long and distinguished military career decided to play a prank on him. As the old soldier walked down the street with his arms full of packages, the jokester sneaked up behind him and shouted, "Attention!" Without hesitation, the military man dropped his arms to his side, and every package went tumbling to the sidewalk. Without a conscious thought, the veteran was doing what comes naturally for a soldier.

Similarly, as believers in Christ, we should respond in a manner that corresponds with our new life. Our behavior is to be more and more in line with the example of Jesus' life. Through faith in Christ we are children of the heavenly Father. By the power of the indwelling Spirit, therefore, let us develop the habit of submitting to God's Word. Then, in every situation of life we will increasingly find that obeying Him is "doing what comes naturally." —R. W. D.

WHEN WE WALK WITH CHRIST, WE BECOME MORE LIKE HIM.

I will never forget Your precepts, for by them You have given me life.

PSALM 119:93

Bible reading and the teaching of Christian values are no longer permitted in many school systems in the Western world. This is not the case in Eastern Europe, however.

Speaking at the American Christian Educators convention in November 1992, a Russian delegate said, "Seventy years ago we closed God out of our country, and it has caused so many problems in our society that we cannot count them. We must put God back into our country, and we must begin with our children."

The deputy of the Ministry of Education said, "Do we have the right to deprive our children of knowledge about God and Christian values? No, and once again, no!"

Getting the Bible back into our individual lives is the first step in getting it back into our classrooms and into society. We must read it regularly, believe what it says, and obey it faithfully. —H. V. L.

TO IGNORE THE BIBLE IS TO INVITE DISASTER.

*Oh, give thanks to the LORD, for He is
good! For His mercy endures forever.*

PSALM 136:1

You don't have to live very long in this world before it
becomes painfully clear that nothing lasts forever. The car
you were so proud of when you bought it is spending too
much time in the shop getting fixed. Those clothes you picked up on
sale are now in the hand-me-down box. At home, the roof eventually
leaks, the appliances break down, the carpet needs to be replaced.

Nothing lasts forever—nothing but God's mercy, that is.
Twenty-six times we are reminded of this inspiring truth in Psalm 136.
Twenty-six times the writer gives us something for which to praise the
Lord, and then he reminds us, "His mercy endures forever."

Think of what this means. When we sin and need forgiveness,
His mercy endures forever. When our lives seem a jumbled mess that
we can't control, His mercy endures forever. Whenever life seems
overwhelming, we can still praise the Lord, as the psalmist did—
for God's mercy is always new and fresh. —J. D. B.

GOD'S HEART IS ALWAYS OVERFLOWING WITH MERCY.

We know that all things work together
for good to those who love God.

ROMANS 8:28

When quoting Romans 8:28, we often begin with the words, "All things work together for good." But the verse really begins like this: "We know that all things work together for good to those who love God." Our knowing comes by faith.

I read a story about a shipwreck. When the sole survivor reached a small, uninhabited island, he prayed for God to rescue him, but help didn't come. Eventually he built a hut out of driftwood for protection from the elements. One day he returned from scavenging for food and found his hut in flames, the smoke rising into the sky. Angrily he cried, "God, how could You do this to me?" The next morning he was awakened by rescuers. "How did you know I was here?" he asked. "We saw your smoke signal," they replied.

The next time it seems as if your last hope has gone up in smoke, remember what "we know" to be true. When God says that all things work together for good to those who love Him, He means all things!
—J. E. Y.

GOD MAY TEST OUR FAITH SO WE MAY TRUST HIS FAITHFULNESS.

He makes my feet like the feet of deer,
and sets me on my high places.
—PSALM 18:33

The bighorn sheep in Colorado's Rocky Mountain National Park will often allow visitors to approach them from below and take close-up photos. But don't try to get above them or the entire herd will run away. The bighorns' escape route from predators is always upward. On level ground a bobcat or cougar can easily overtake the wild sheep, but scrambling up a boulder-strewn slope, the bighorns will get away every time.

Years ago I heard a speaker say, "No matter what danger you face from trouble or temptation, don't let it get between you and God." As Christians, our escape route is always upward toward the Lord, never downward into sin or self-pity.

The psalmist's words remind us how to keep difficulty on the downhill side: "My voice You shall hear in the morning, O LORD; in the morning I will direct it to You, and I will look up" (Ps. 5:3). Then, in a beautiful word picture, David described how God answered his prayer for help: "He makes my feet like the feet of deer, and sets me on my high places" (Ps. 18:33). —D. C. M.

YOU CAN BE SURE OF YOUR FOOTING WHEN
YOU WALK CLOSE TO JESUS.

*As long as he lives he shall be lent to the L*ORD.

1 SAMUEL 1:28

When Hannah dedicated Samuel to God, she meant business. She didn't just take him to the temple for dedication; she left him there. She turned him over to Eli to bring him up in God's service.

As I listened to a preacher talk about Hannah's commitment, I began to wonder who gets our children today? Samuel was continually taught and instructed by Eli in God's temple. Who teaches our kids?

Is it TV and movies? How many hours of instruction does the electronic mass media give them each day?

Is it school? Do we know what is going on in the classroom? Are there any philosophies we need to combat?

Is it the Lord? How much time and effort do we spend to make sure our children know that a relationship with the Lord is the basis for security, peace, and contentment? —J. D. B.

IF CHILDREN ARE TO FIND THE WAY TO
GOD, PARENTS MUST POINT THE WAY.

The blood of Jesus Christ His Son cleanses us from all sin.

1 JOHN 1:7

When evangelist John Wesley (1703–1791) was returning home from a service one night, he was robbed. The thief, however, found his victim to have only a little money and some Christian literature.

As the bandit was leaving, Wesley called out, "Stop! I have something more to give you." The surprised robber paused. "My friend," said Wesley, "you may live to regret this sort of life. If you ever do, here's something to remember: 'The blood of Jesus Christ cleanses us from all sin!'" The thief hurried away, and Wesley prayed that his words might bear fruit.

Years later, Wesley was greeting people after a Sunday service when he was approached by a stranger. What a surprise to learn that this visitor, now a believer in Christ and a successful businessman, was the one who had robbed him years before! "I owe it all to you," said the transformed man. "Oh no, my friend," Wesley exclaimed, "not to me, but to the precious blood of Christ that cleanses us from all sin!"
—H. G. B.

THE GOSPEL IS A PRICELESS GIFT TO BE FREELY GIVEN TO OTHERS.

Where your treasure is, there your heart will be also.

MATTHEW 6:21

Some evening when you have a spare moment, get out your old checkbook registers and read through the entries. You may find it interesting, and perhaps somewhat startling, to discover just how the money you've earned has been spent.

The entries will read like a family history book. They chronicle every major event—births, deaths, and illnesses—and quite accurately reflect your tastes, habits, and interests.

They record your vacations, travels, and other moves. They also tell much about how expensively you dress or how extravagantly you eat. The total spent in each category will pinpoint the things that make the greatest demands on your income— either because of need or by choice.

Such a checkbook checkup might also show our spiritual temperature. The contributions given to the work of the Lord compared with the expenditures for the unnecessary things of life offer some clues.

Try doing a checkbook checkup today. —R. W. D.

WE SHOW WHAT WE LOVE BY WHAT WE DO WITH WHAT WE HAVE.

It is good to sing praises to our God.

PSALM 147:1

I understand why I've never been asked to join a choir or sing a solo. Musical talent is not one of my gifts. I discovered this at 9 years of age when I was outside one day singing lustily. My mother opened the door and asked, "Is one of the calves sick? I think I just heard one."

My mother's words have never kept me from praising God in song, however. And when I preach somewhere, I enthusiastically join in congregational singing (making sure, of course, not to stand too close to the microphone).

God's great salvation fills me with gratitude, and one way to express my joy is to sing about it. That's why I'm puzzled by people who say they are Christians but admit that they seldom attend church services, almost never listen to Christian music, and find singing hymns and listening to sermons boring. I can understand nonbelievers saying this because they know neither God nor the joy of salvation. But believers do! —H. V. L.

A HEART IN TUNE WITH GOD WILL SING HIS PRAISE.

Moses' hands became heavy. . . .
And Aaron and Hur supported his hands.

EXODUS 17:12

In 1989, paraplegic Mark Wellman climbed the sheer granite face of Yosemite's El Capitan. On the last day of his climb, *The Fresno Bee* ran a picture of Wellman being carried triumphantly on the shoulders of climbing companion Mike Corbett. The caption read, "Paraplegic and partner prove no wall is too high to climb." What the story did not say is that in helping Wellman scale El Capitan once, Corbett had to make that difficult, demanding ascent three times!

Today's Bible reading focuses on Moses, whose upheld hands brought God's help in a crucial battle. But don't forget Aaron and Hur. They had to climb the same mountain themselves, and their support of Moses' arms took time, strength, and commitment on their part. The principle is this: People who serve the Lord "behind the scenes" often pay a higher price than those who are in the center of public attention. —D. C. E.

WE NEED EACH OTHER IF WE ARE TO
DO WHAT GOD WANTS US TO DO.

[God] predestined us to adoption as sons by Jesus Christ to Himself.

EPHESIANS 1:5

Penelope Duckworth, a chaplain at Stanford University, talked with a Christian woman who had adopted a Jewish daughter. She explained that after Hitler had annexed Poland, the Nazis came to her village to round up Jews. She had been shopping near the train station where German soldiers were loading Jews into rail cars. Those helpless victims were destined to die in a concentration camp.

That woman saw a soldier pushing a Jewess toward the station, and she had a little girl toddling behind. He stopped her and demanded, "Is she your daughter?" The terrified mother looked straight into the Christian woman's eyes, who then was standing nearby and said, "No, the child is hers." From that moment the Christian woman took that Jewish girl as her own daughter.

By grace God has claimed us for His own. We were condemned, not as innocent victims, but justly as sinners. We were once alienated; now by faith adopted! —V. C. G.

GOD CLAIMS BY GRACE THOSE WHO HAVE NO CLAIM TO GRACE.

They continued steadfastly in the apostles' doctrine and fellowship.

ACTS 2:42

In his book *Why Christians Sin,* J. Kirk Johnston tells about a young Russian woman who, before the collapse of the Iron Curtain, was allowed to visit her relatives in Canada. She was a devout Christian, and her friends assumed that she would defect and seek asylum in Canada or the US because of the religious oppression in the USSR. But they were wrong. She wanted to go back to her homeland.

This Russian woman said that people in the West were too busy acquiring material things and not concerned enough about their relationships. In her homeland, Christian fellowship was essential to their faith because it provided the support and encouragement they so desperately needed.

Genuine Christian fellowship involves much more than visiting over a cup of coffee in the church kitchen. It is loving one another, caring for one another, bearing one another's burdens. —R. W. D.

CHRISTIAN FELLOWSHIP IS ESSENTIAL TO SPIRITUAL GROWTH.

Search me, O God, and know my heart.

PSALM 139:23

Years ago, a radio station received a letter from a sheepherder who lived on an isolated ranch in the western part of the United States. Never before had the station received such an unusual request. It read, "Will you please strike 'A' on the piano in your studio? I am far from a piano, and the only comfort I have is my fiddle. Just now it is out of tune. Will you strike 'A' so that I can get it in tune again?"

That is a picture of us when our lives get out of tune with the Savior. The strings of moral conviction, once finely attuned to God's Word, become loose through compromise or neglect. Daily we need to make sure we are in harmony with God. The Spirit through the Word gives us the sure note to which we can tune our lives. —D. J. D.

**WHEN THE HEART IS IN TUNE WITH CHRIST,
THE DISCORDS OF LIFE BECOME HARMONIOUS.**

Great peace have those who love Your law.

PSALM 120:165

A philosophy professor began each new term by asking his class, "Do you believe it can be shown that there are absolute values like justice?" The free-thinking students all argued that everything is relative and no single law can be applied universally. Before the end of the semester, the professor devoted one class period to debate the issue. At the end, he concluded, "Regardless of what you think, I want you to know that absolute values can be demonstrated. And if you don't accept what I say, I'll flunk you!" One angry student got up and insisted, "That's not fair!" "You've just proved my point," replied the professor. "You've appealed to a higher standard of fairness."

God's moral standards are in the Bible, and He has given us a conscience to tell us right from wrong (Rom. 2:14–15). Every time we use the words *good* and *bad*, we imply a standard by which we make such judgments. Biblical values are not outdated. They are good for any age because they originate with an eternal, unchanging God.

—D. J. D.

ONLY GOD HAS THE RIGHT TO SAY WHAT'S WRONG.

Come aside by yourselves to a deserted place and rest a while.

MARK 6:31

According to tradition, when the apostle John was overseer in Ephesus, his hobby was raising pigeons. It is said that on one occasion another elder passed his house as he returned from hunting and saw John playing with one of his birds. The man gently chided him for spending his time so frivolously. John looked at the hunter's bow and remarked that the string was loose. "Yes," said the elder, "I always loosen the string of my bow when it's not in use. If it stayed tight, it would lose its resilience and fail me in the hunt." John responded, "And I am now relaxing the bow of my mind so that I may be better able to shoot the arrows of divine truth."

We cannot do our best work with nerves taut or frayed from being constantly under pressure. When Jesus' disciples returned from a strenuous preaching mission, their Master recognized their need for rest and invited them to come with Him to a quiet place where they could be refreshed. Jesus invites you too. —D. J. D.

IF WE ARE TO FUNCTION AT OUR BEST, TIME IS NEEDED FOR REST.

Behold, I stand at the door and knock.

REVELATION 3:20

*I*t took years before she finally said "yes." A Welshman had fallen in love with one of his neighbors and wanted to marry her. But they had quarreled, and she refused to forgive. Shy and reluctant to face the offended woman, the persistent suitor slipped a love letter under her door every week.

At last, after 42 years, he summoned up courage, knocked on her door, and asked her to become his wife. To his surprise and delight, she consented. So they were married at the age of 74!

God is also a persistent lover. Century after century He sent prophets as His messengers beseeching the stubborn, alienated people of Israel to live with Him, a faithful covenant-keeper. But all those overtures were sinfully refused. Then at Bethlehem, God Himself came in the Person of Jesus Christ. Now, having opened up the way for reconciliation by His redeeming sacrifice at Calvary, He stands at the door of everyone's heart, knocking and asking all to accept Him.

—V. C. G.

GOD ALWAYS KNOCKS LOUD ENOUGH FOR A WILLING SOUL TO HEAR.

It is good for me that I have been afflicted.

PSALM 119:71

I heard a story about a man who was deep in debt. On his way to work each day, he walked past the door of a wealthy businessman. When the rich man learned of the debtor's plight, he decided to help him.

So one day as the poor man walked by, the wealthy man threw a heavy bag out the door and unintentionally struck him, slightly injuring him. When he picked up the bag, he heard the clinking of coins. Opening it, he was amazed to find that there was more than enough money to pay off his debt. Just then he heard a voice call out from the businessman's door: "Keep it. It's yours."

Sometimes life's troubles hit us like that heavy bag, knocking us down and causing us injury. But God can bring great gain into our lives through our burdens and trials. Rather than questioning God and grumbling at the burdens He allows, reaffirm your trust in His goodness. You'll discover that burdens are actually blessings in disguise. —P. R. V.

THANKING GOD IN YOUR TRIALS TURNS BURDENS INTO BLESSINGS.

Why do you look at the speck in your brother's eye,
but do not perceive the plank in your own eye?

LUKE 6:41

John was driving home late one night when he picked up a hitchhiker. As they rode along, he began to be suspicious of his passenger. John checked to see if his wallet was safe in the pocket of his coat that was on the seat between them, but it wasn't there! So he slammed on the brakes, ordered the hitchhiker out, and said, "Hand over the wallet immediately!" The frightened hitchhiker handed over a billfold, and John drove off. When he arrived home, he started to tell his wife about the experience, but she interrupted him, saying, "Before I forget, John, do you know that you left your wallet at home this morning?"

Let's be careful not to form our opinions about others until we have all the facts. Instead, we should first take an honest look at ourselves. Many unkind words have been spoken and many relationships have been hurt because someone was too quick to judge another person. How important it is not to jump to conclusions! —H. G. B.

PEOPLE WHO JUMP TO CONCLUSIONS OFTEN LAND ON A LIE.

*By grace you have been saved through
faith . . . ; it is the gift of God.*

EPHESIANS 2:8

During the Spanish-American War, Clara Barton was overseeing the work of the Red Cross in Cuba. One day Colonel Theodore Roosevelt came to her, wanting to buy food for his sick and wounded Rough Riders. But she refused to sell him any.

Roosevelt was perplexed. His men needed the help and he was prepared to pay out of his own funds. When he asked someone why he could not buy the supplies, he was told, "Colonel, just ask for it!" A smile broke over Roosevelt's face. Now he understood—the provisions were not for sale. All he had to do was simply ask and they would be given freely.

That's how a sinner receives eternal life. Salvation is a gift. If it could be bought at an auction, millionaires would compete for the purchase and most people would be excluded. If it could be gained by working for it, the strong would push the weak out of the running. But God's forgiveness is free for the asking. Nothing we can do will ever earn it. —P. R. V.

WHY PAY THE HIGH PRICE OF BEING LOST WHEN SALVATION IS FREE?

Lay up for yourselves treasures in heaven.

MATTHEW 6:20

George W. Truett, a well-known pastor, was invited to dinner in the home of a very wealthy man in Texas. After the meal, the host led him to a place where they could get a good view of the surrounding area.

Pointing to the oil wells punctuating the landscape, he boasted, "Twenty-five years ago I had nothing. Now, as far as you can see, it's all mine." Looking in the opposite direction at his sprawling fields of grain, he said, "That's all mine." Turning east toward huge herds of cattle, he bragged, "They're all mine." Then, pointing to the west and a beautiful forest, he exclaimed, "That too is all mine."

He paused, expecting Dr. Truett to compliment him on his great success. Truett, however, placing one hand on the man's shoulder and pointing heavenward with the other, simply said, "How much do you have in that direction?" The man hung his head and confessed, "I never thought of that."

The wise investor lays up treasure in heaven. —R. W. D.

YOU CAN'T TAKE IT WITH YOU, BUT YOU CAN SEND IT ON AHEAD.

Having been justified by faith, we have peace with God.

ROMANS 5:1

As a kid I played a game called "Aggravation." To win, you had to be the first to get your four marbles from start to finish. But if an opponent's marble landed on a space occupied by one of yours, you had to go back to the beginning and start all over.

That's how some Christians view their relationship with God. They believe that they advance in their Christian life until they sin, then they have to start all over. Yet if that were true, we could never be secure in our relationship to Christ, for we all sin every day.

When we sin, we don't need to go back and start all over again—just repent and keep on going. —D. C. E.

**JUSTIFICATION MEANS OUR GUILT
GONE, CHRIST'S GOODNESS GIVEN.**

We love Him because He first loved us.

1 JOHN 4:19

Nansen, the Norwegian explorer, tried to measure an extremely deep part of the Arctic ocean. The first day, he used his longest measuring line but couldn't reach bottom. He wrote in his log book, "The ocean is deeper than that!"

The next day, he added more line but still could not measure the depth, and so again in his record book he wrote, "Deeper than that!" After several days of adding more and more pieces of rope and cord to his line, he had to leave that part of the ocean without learning its actual depth. All he knew was that it was beyond his ability to measure.

So too, we cannot plumb the depths of God's love. Our human measuring line is too short. God will take all eternity to show us the fullness of His love. Both now and forever, as we try to comprehend God's love, we may well exclaim, "It's deeper—much deeper than that!" —H. G. B.

GOD'S LOVE KNOWS NO BOUNDS.

With us is the LORD our God, to help us and to fight our battles.

2 CHRONICLES 32:8

The citizens of Feldkirch, Austria, didn't know what to do. Napoleon's massive army was preparing to attack. Soldiers had been spotted on the heights above the little town, which was situated on the Austrian border. So a council of citizens was hastily summoned to decide whether they should try to defend themselves or display the white flag of surrender. It happened to be Easter Sunday, and the people had gathered in the local church.

The pastor rose and said, "Friends, we have been counting on our own strength, and apparently that has failed. As this is the day of our Lord's resurrection, let us just ring the bells, have our services as usual, and leave the matter in His hands."

The council accepted his plan and the church bells rang. The enemy, hearing the sudden peal, concluded that the Austrian army had arrived during the night to defend the town. Before the service ended, the enemy broke camp and left.

We too may be facing circumstances that threaten to crush us. But let us call out to the Lord and depend on His almighty power.

—H. G. B.

TRUST IN GOD'S POWER PREVENTS PANIC.

I pray that your love may abound still more and more.

PHILIPPIANS 1:9

It is said that one day Michelangelo entered his studio to examine the work of his students. As he came to the painting of one of his favorite pupils, he stood and looked at it for a long time. Then, to the utter surprise of the class, he suddenly took a brush and wrote one word across the canvas.

That one word he splashed on the picture was *amplius,* meaning "larger." Michelangelo was not rejecting the work, for it exhibited great skill and was good as far as it went. But the small size of the canvas had made its design appear cramped. It needed to be expanded.

The Lord may have to write the word *amplius* across many of our lives. Our spiritual outlook becomes confined, and our vision of what God wants to do in and through us gets restricted by our small faith and limited spiritual growth. He wants to increase the dimensions of our spiritual lives, widen our outreach, and strengthen our witness. —P. R. V.

OUR LIMITED VISION NEEDS CONTINUAL REVISION.

Whoever believes in [Jesus] should not perish but have eternal life.

JOHN 3:15

What a night for the Minnesota Twins baseball team in 1987! They had just defeated the Detroit Tigers and won the American League pennant for the first time in 22 years. More than 50,000 people, young and old, crowded into the Metrodome to welcome their victors home from Detroit. Banners were waving, horns were blaring, the crowd was cheering. There were even tears of joy.

The players were surrounded by members of the news media. One reporter in the crowd called out to Greg Gagne, the Twins' star shortstop, and commented, "This has got to be the greatest moment of your life." Quietly Gagne replied, "Actually, no. That was the moment I asked Jesus Christ into my life."

We enjoy high moments when some hard-won goal has been reached or a victory has been achieved. But as Christians, we realize that our times of triumph are less than dust compared with the moment we accepted Jesus Christ as our Savior. It's a decision that changes our destiny forever (John 3:15–16). —V. C. G.

WHAT YOU DECIDE ABOUT CHRIST DETERMINES YOUR DESTINY.

No longer do I call you servants, . . . but I have called you friends.

JOHN 15:15

Rene Lacoste, the world's top tennis player in the late 1920s, won seven major singles titles during his career, including multiple victories at Wimbledon, the US Open, and the French Open. His friends called him "Le Crocodile," an apt term for his tenacious play on the court.

Lacoste accepted the nickname and had a tiny crocodile embroidered on his tennis blazer. When he added it to a line of shirts he designed, the symbol caught on. While thousands of people around the world wore "alligator shirts," the emblem always had a deeper significance for Lacoste's friends who knew its origin and meaning.

The cross, an emblem of Christianity, holds special meaning for every friend of Christ. Whenever we see a cross, it speaks to us of Christ's tenacious determination to do His Father's will by dying for us on Calvary. What a privilege to know Him and be included in His words to His disciples: "No longer do I call you servants, . . . but I have called you friends." —D. C. M.

**BECAUSE OF THE CROSS OF CHRIST,
WE CAN BECOME FRIENDS OF CHRIST.**

Your law . . . is my meditation all the day.

PSALM 119:97

*M*editation on God's Word doesn't have to end when your devotional time is over. You can continue the blessing by taking Scripture with you throughout the day.

Some people memorize a passage or write it on a card so they can have it available to read when they get a few moments. An engineer uses his coffee breaks to continue his reflection on God's Word. Homemakers attach verses to the refrigerator or bathroom mirror. Truckers put portions of the Bible on their dashboard.

Leslie B. Flynn tells of a brilliant college student who volunteered to work at a church camp and ended up as the designated potato peeler. A friend who admired her intelligence said, "It's too bad you had to end up peeling potatoes." She replied, "I don't have to think about potatoes while I'm peeling them. So I think about my Bible verse for the day."

When the Word of God is in our minds from morning to night, we'll be more likely to obey it and far less likely to violate it. That's the value of ongoing meditation. —D. C. E.

**READING THE BIBLE WITHOUT MEDITATING
ON IT IS LIKE EATING WITHOUT CHEWING.**

*He shall be like a tree planted by the rivers of
water, that brings forth its fruit in its season.*

PSALM 1:3

People who don't want to wait 4 decades for a globe
Norway maple to grow in their front yard can buy a 30-foot
specimen from a New York nursery for $42,000. A 50-foot European
beech is a "bargain" for only $20,000. In spite of the prices, the
country's leading nurseries report soaring sales of mature trees.

As one customer put it: "I can't wait for a banana to ripen. I only
buy them bright yellow. There's no patience for watching a tree grow."

We humans are always in a hurry, looking for shortcuts to skirt
the process and grasp the product. And sometimes we expect instant
maturity in our Christian walk and growth in faith. What a contrast
to the enormous leisure of God in His dealings with us!

If our roots are in God's Word and our hearts are drawing
sustenance from Him, we will flourish. And growth toward maturity
brings joy to the God of patience. —D. C. M.

IT TAKES A MOMENT TO BE SAVED;
IT TAKES A LIFETIME TO GROW IN GODLINESS.

God . . . has begotten us . . . to an
inheritance . . . reserved in heaven.

1 PETER 1:3–4

When Mike Peters won the 1981 Pulitzer Prize for political cartoons, he wasn't expecting the honor. He described his response by saying, "It is like you are asleep and it is 2 in the morning and you are hugging your pillow and you are in your funny pajamas and somebody bursts through the door and they come over and start shaking you and they say, 'Wake up, wake up!' And you say, 'What is it?' And they say, 'You have just won the Boston Marathon!' And you say, 'But I'm not running in the Boston Marathon.' And they say, 'Doesn't make any difference, you won.'"

Jesus taught that heaven too will hold some surprises. Honor and glory will be granted for behavior that was so natural, so undistinguished, and so noncompetitive. Many of God's children will be surprised to find that their faithful service has brought them top honors. —M. R .D. II

WORK DONE WELL FOR CHRIST WILL RECEIVE A "WELL DONE" FROM CHRIST.

Put on the whole armor of God, that you may be
able to stand against the wiles of the devil.

EPHESIANS 6:11

In an article for *Youth Ministries* magazine, a 14-year veteran of the Navy SEALs describes the color-code system they use to indicate levels of combat readiness. Each stage has a parallel in spiritual warfare.

Condition White: The soldier is relaxed and daydreaming, unaware of his surroundings. A Christian in this condition is easy prey for Satan.

Condition Yellow: The soldier is relaxed physically but alert mentally. A believer at this level may sense trouble coming, but he's not ready to confront it.

Condition Orange: The soldier is physically prepared, mentally alert, and ready to fight. A believer at this stage has on the full armor of God.

Condition Red: As in condition orange, the soldier is ready to fight. The difference is experience. A battle-seasoned Christian knows quickly what to do because of his experience and familiarity with Scripture.

If we stay alert and armed, we can fend off Satan's most powerful attacks. —D. C. E.

SPIRITUAL VICTORY COMES ONLY TO THOSE
WHO ARE PREPARED FOR BATTLE.

The righteousness of the blameless will direct his way aright.

PROVERBS 11:5

My daughter was coming home from college for the weekend to play the piano at her friend's wedding. Before she left, I sent her an e-mail directing her to take an alternate route instead of the one she usually travels for the 6-hour drive home. Why? Because on that road a few weeks earlier my wife and I had been delayed for 2 hours by construction crews.

As parents, we must provide alternate routes in life as well. We've observed the wrong highways others have traveled or perhaps the foolish ways we have taken, and we know they lead to delay or danger.

Think of all the possible paths our children might choose—the road of sexual immorality, the avenue of alcohol and drug abuse, the way of ungodly friends. But in Christ, there is an alternate path—a route that will lead our children away from the struggles we know they'll face on any other road. Let's model it clearly. —J. D. B.

THE RIGHT WAY STARTS WITH THE WAY OF THE CROSS.

Eat honey because it is good, and the
honeycomb which is sweet to your taste.

PROVERBS 24:13

The absent-minded professor strode into his freshman zoology class with a paper bag in his hand and a twinkle in his eye. His broad grin projected the delight he felt in knowing he was about to initiate his rather squeamish students in the methods of animal dissection. In his typical professorial style he proudly announced, "I have brought a frog, fresh from the pond, that we might together study its outer appearance and later dissect it." With that he opened the bag and carefully unwrapped the contents. To his complete puzzlement, there was a ham-on-rye sandwich. "That's strange," he said. "I distinctly remember eating my lunch."

Are we careful what our minds feed on? Is what we take into our minds pure and true and honoring to God? We must be careful that our lives are not marked by an absent-mindedness that we will someday regret. —M. R. D. II

IF YOU DON'T WANT THE FRUITS OF SIN,
STAY OUT OF THE DEVIL'S ORCHARD.

The LORD shall preserve your going out and your coming in.

PSALM 121:8

Psalm 121 was a favorite of my father. Scottish people called it "The Traveler's Psalm." Whenever a family member, a guest, or a friend was leaving on a journey, this psalm was read— or more often sung—at family prayers. When my father left the "old country" as a teenager to sail alone to the United States, he was bidden farewell with this psalm.

Over the years, my father enjoyed many hearty days but endured others that were dark and grim. In World War I, he carried this psalm's words with him into battle, and then out of it as he lay in a hospital for almost a year recovering from shrapnel wounds.

In verse 1, the psalmist looked beyond the hills to the God who made them. My father lived in the toughest section of New York City. Although he seldom saw hills, he held to the assurance that the God of the hills was also the God of the dangerous city streets. —H. W. R.

KEEP YOUR EYES ON GOD; HE NEVER TAKES HIS EYES OFF YOU.

In Him we have redemption . . . according to the riches of His grace.

EPHESIANS 1:7

Last year I visited Niagara Falls for the first time and was awed by the sight and sound and overpowering sense of it all. Every minute, about 200,000 tons of water plunge into the Niagara River gorge in a thunderous ovation to the lavish, generous nature of God.

The Lord could have used a lot less water, but He didn't. He could have made the falls lower, but He built them 12 stories high. And because they are what they are from the creative hand of God, people come from all over the world to see Niagara Falls.

What a picture of God's grace in Jesus Christ! "In Him we have redemption . . . according to the riches of His grace which He made to *abound* toward us" (Eph. 1:7–8). The Greek word translated *abound* means "an exceeding measure, something above the ordinary." God's grace toward us is not squeezed out from an eye-dropper or carefully rationed. His grace is a Niagara of superabundance so lavish that we marvel at its display. —D. C. M.

GOD'S HEART IS ALWAYS OVERFLOWING WITH GRACE.

*In everything give thanks; for this is the
will of God in Christ Jesus for you.*

1 THESSALONIANS 5:18

At harvest time it's natural to thank God for the bounty of His blessings. The Feast of Weeks in ancient Israel, established in Leviticus 23, was a week of joyous celebration and feasting in gratitude for the harvest (Deut. 16:9–12). Even today as farmers gather their crops, many give thanks to the Lord for the abundance of their harvest.

But what if untimely and persistent rain keeps the farmer from getting his machines into the fields and harvesting the ripe grain? What if a sudden hailstorm flattens the corn? Or a summer drought dries up the fields?

The apostle Paul wrote, "In everything give thanks" (1 Thess. 5:18). That may sound unrealistic. But think about it. The Jews were instructed to celebrate the Feast of Weeks whether the crops came in or not. Likewise, we are to give thanks to the Lord "in everything." —D. C. E.

**WE DON'T NEED MORE TO BE THANKFUL
FOR, WE NEED TO BE MORE THANKFUL.**

*For I say . . . to everyone . . . not to think
of himself more highly than he ought.*

ROMANS 12:3

A man who had just been elected to the British
Parliament brought his family to London and was giving
them a tour of the city. When they entered Westminster Abbey, his
eight-year-old daughter seemed awestruck by the size and beauty of
that magnificent structure. Her proud father, curious about what was
going on in her mind, asked, "And what, my child, are you thinking
about?" She replied, "Daddy, I was just thinking about how big you
are in our house, but how small you look here!"

One thing that stands out in the Word of God is that the
Lord despises the haughty. Under inspiration the psalmist said, "One
who has a haughty look and a proud heart, him I will not endure"
(Ps. 101:5). If we ask the Holy Spirit to help us see ourselves as we
really are, He will enable us to control our foolish pride. —R. W. D.

THOSE WHO KNOW GOD WILL BE HUMBLE.

Your heavenly Father knows that you need all these things.

MATTHEW 6:32

In Bristol, England, George Müller operated an orphanage for two thousand children. One evening, knowing they had no food for breakfast the next morning, Müller called his workers together and explained the situation. After two or three prayed, Müller said, "That is sufficient. Let us rise and praise God for prayer answered." The next morning they could not push open the great front door. To see what was holding it closed, they went out the back door and around the building. Stacked up against the front door were boxes filled with food. One of the workers later remarked, "We know Who sent the baskets, but we do not know who brought them!"

God uses many messengers and means to deliver His gifts, whether they are material or spiritual provisions. We may not always recognize that His hand is working behind the scenes, but it is.

—P. R. V.

GOD OFTEN SENDS HIS HELP BY WAY OF HUMAN HANDS.

Holy, holy, holy, is the LORD of hosts.

ISAIAH 6:3

1. As a holy God, He is perfect in His righteousness. We can fully surrender to His will, because we are confident that He will always do with us what is right (Gen. 18:25).
2. As a holy God, He is perfect in His justice. We can know that His judgment will be unquestionably fair (2 Cor. 5:10).
3. As a holy God, He is perfect in His faithfulness. We can take Him at His Word (Num. 23:19).
4. As a holy God, He is perfect in His truthfulness. We can depend on Him. He will never let us down (Lam. 3:22–23).

We can have absolute confidence in our righteous, just, truthful, and faithful God. He is holy. —R. W. D.

THE HOLINESS OF GOD THAT CONVICTS THE SINNER COMFORTS THE SAINT.

Let us run with endurance the race that
is set before us, looking unto Jesus.

HEBREWS 12:1–2

In *The Complete Disciple,* Paul W. Powell describes a picture of a rugged wagon train painted by a famous artist of the American West. It is night, and the wagons have been drawn into a circle for protection. The men are gathered around the campfire, and the wagon-master has a map spread out before him. On the map a heavy black line traces the zigzag course they have followed. They had swung north a little, then south, but always toward the west. An argument seems to have erupted about which way to go next. But the leader, with weary determination, has placed one finger on the end of the black line. With his other arm he is pointing toward the shadowy mountains. He seems to be saying, "We may have to go south around a mountain, or north across a river, but our direction will always be west."

Every Christian should have a similar resolve. Difficult circumstances may stand in our way as we continue on the course God has marked out. But if we keep our eyes on the goal by "looking unto Jesus," we will not stray from the path He has outlined. —D. C. E.

AN OBSTACLE CANNOT STOP US IF
WE KEEP OUR EYES ON THE GOAL.

You will forget the shame of your youth.

ISAIAH 54:4

Two men walking down a country road decided to take a shortcut home. They passed through a field where a number of cattle were grazing. Deeply engrossed in conversation when they reached the other side of the pasture, they forgot to shut the gate behind them. A few minutes later one of them noticed the oversight and ran back to close the gate. As he did, he remembered the last words of an old friend who summoned all his children to his bedside and gave them this wise counsel: "As you travel down life's pathway, remember to close the gates behind you."

The man knew that problems, difficult situations, heartbreaks, and failures were inevitable, but he wanted his children to know that they didn't have to allow those things to follow them through life.

This is especially true for believers. Once we have confessed a sin and have done what we can to right the wrong, we must put the incident behind us. —R. W. D.

WE INVITE DEFEAT WHEN WE REMEMBER WHAT WE SHOULD FORGET.

Wrath kills a foolish man, and envy slays a simple one.

JOB 5:2

On the wall of a chapel in Padua, an old city in northeastern Italy, hangs a painting by the Renaissance artist Giotto. The painter depicted Envy with long ears that could hear every bit of news of another's success. He also gave to Envy the tongue of a serpent to poison the reputation of the one being envied. But if you could look at the painting carefully, you would notice that the tongue coils back and stings the eyes of the figure itself. Not only did Giotto picture Envy as being blind, but also as destroying itself with its own venomous evil.

If we resent the success and accomplishments of others and find ourselves striking out at them with damaging words or insidious innuendoes, we have a problem with jealousy. But God wants to administer the antidote of love. That alone will keep us from becoming jealousy's victim. —D. C. E.

**IF WE SHOOT ARROWS OF JEALOUSY
AT OTHERS, WE WOUND OURSELVES.**

Preserve me, O God, for in You I put my trust.

PSALM 16:1

Some people touring a mint where coins are made came to the smelting area. As they stood before the caldrons filled with molten metal, the tour guide explained that if a person were to dip his hand into water and then have someone pour the hot liquid over his hand, he would neither be injured nor feel any pain. Picking out one couple, he asked if they would like to prove what he had just said. "No, thank you," the husband quickly said. "I'll take your word for it." But his wife responded eagerly. "Sure, I'll give it a try." Matching action to her words, she thrust her hand into a bucket of water and then held it out as the molten metal was poured over it. The hot liquid rolled off harmlessly just as the guide had said it would. The host turned to the husband and remarked, "Sir, you claimed to believe what I said. But your wife truly trusted."

If we only claim to believe God's promises but never act on them, we will miss out on His marvelous blessings. —R. W. D.

TO TRUST IS TO TRIUMPH.

Create in me a clean heart, O God.

PSALM 51:10

God can bring good out of our failures, and even out of our sins. J. Stuart Holden tells of an old Scottish mansion close to where he had his summer home. The walls of one room were covered by sketches made by distinguished artists. The practice began after a pitcher of soda water, spilled accidentally on a freshly decorated wall, left an unsightly stain. At the time, a noted artist, Lord Landseer, was a guest in the house. One day when the family went to the moors, he stayed behind. With a few masterful strokes of a piece of charcoal, the ugly spot became the outline of a beautiful waterfall, bordered by trees and wildlife. The artist turned a disfigured wall into one of his best depictions of Highland life.

God never condones sin, nor does He spare His chastening rod. But when we confess, He begins a new work in our hearts. He does more than the artist did with the stain on the wall. God removes the blot of sin entirely and cleanses us. —P. R. V.

AS LONG AS WE HAVE THE GRACE OF GOD, FAILURE IS NOT FINAL.

Make a joyful shout to the LORD, . . .
come before His presence with singing.

PSALM 100:1–2

An old Jewish legend says that after God had created the world He called the angels to Himself and asked them what they thought of it. One of them said, "The only thing lacking is the sound of praise to the Creator." So God created music, and it was heard in the whisper of the wind and in the song of the birds. He also gave man the gift of song. And throughout all the ages, music has blessed multitudes of people.

Music is one of those good things in life we take for granted. Yet it is a blessing from the Lord. It soothes troubled hearts and motivates us to live for Christ. And through it we lift our hearts in praise to the Lord.

When we join voices with fellow believers and lift our hearts in hymns of praise, we honor the Lord, edify our brothers and sisters in Christ, and bring joy to our own lives. —R. W. D.

NO MUSIC SO PLEASES GOD AS THE
HEARTFELT PRAISES OF HIS SAINTS.

This is the day the Lord has made; we will rejoice and be glad in it.

PSALM 118:24

Blind and deaf from the age of two, Helen Keller was asked by a young boy, "Isn't it the worst thing in the world to be blind?" Smiling, she replied, "Not half so bad as to have two good eyes and see nothing."

Many people with sharp eyesight and acute hearing seem totally unaware of the beautiful sights and pleasing sounds all around them. They never notice the majesty of stately trees, the tranquility of a quiet lake, or the splendor of starry skies. They fail to hear the melodies of singing birds or the gentle rustling of leaves.

God is pleased when we delight in the wonders of His creation and praise Him for them. Stepping outside each morning and breathing the fresh air reminds us to stop a moment and thank God for life. And an approaching storm with its flashing lightning and rolling thunder displays the power of God, prompting us to worship. Observing the sights and sounds around us will motivate us to live for the Lord and to praise Him. —H. V. L.

LEARN TO ENJOY NATURE'S BEAUTY—IT'S THE HANDWRITING OF GOD.

Now give me wisdom and knowledge.

2 CHRONICLES 1:10

When offered one wish, Midas, a legendary Phrygian king, asked that all he touched might turn to gold. His golden desire granted, Midas realized as soon as he wanted to eat that the gift was a curse, not a blessing. Although he got what he wanted, he didn't want what he got.

King Solomon also was offered one wish. But he did not waste it on a selfish, greedy request. Instead, he asked for wisdom that he might judge God's people justly. In requesting wisdom above riches, Solomon revealed right reasons for wanting to be wise. He asked not for his own benefit.

Wise people know how to learn; they never seek knowledge for their own sake. They know how to talk; they speak the truth in love. They know how to act; they pursue justice to evade evil. They balance their words and actions. They say and do the right things at the right time for the right reasons. —D. J. D.

THEY ARE WISE WHO TAKE GOD FOR A TEACHER.

Behold, the eye of the LORD is on those who fear Him.

PSALM 33:18

William Cowper, though a Christian, had sunk to the depths of despair. One foggy night he called for a horsedrawn carriage and asked to be taken to the London Bridge on the Thames River. He was so overcome by depression that he intended to commit suicide. After two hours of driving through the mist, Cowper's coachman reluctantly confessed that he was lost. Disgusted by the delay, Cowper left the carriage and decided to find the London Bridge on foot. After walking a short distance, he discovered that he was at his own doorstep. The carriage had been going in circles. Recognizing the restraining hand of God and convicted by the Spirit, Cowper realized that the way out of his troubles was to look to God, not to jump into the river. With gratitude he sat down and wrote these reassuring words: "God moves in a mysterious way His wonders to perform; He plants His footsteps in the sea, and rides upon the storm."

God's eye is always on His children, and our needs are His concern. —H. G. B.

NO LIFE IS HOPELESS UNLESS CHRIST IS RULED OUT.

Be my rock of refuge . . . and my fortress.

PSALM 31:2–3

*P*rotection comes in many forms. A rabbit dives for his hole. A squirrel clings to the backside of a branch. A deer runs for the dense cover of a swamp. A two-year-old runs for his dad's pant-leg. A teenager looks for the security of friends. A marine digs in under cover of friendly guns. But what does a Christian do? Where do we hide when surrounded by danger?

David had the answer to that question. When he wrote Psalm 31, things were not going well for him. He was hurting, tired, and weak. His mind was distressed, his heart broken. His enemies were chasing him, and his friends had let him down. Though vulnerable, he was not defenseless. He knew that in God is the safest place, and that the wisest defense strategy is having a right relationship with Him. So that's where he found his security. He called upon the name of God.

—M. R. D. II

CHRISTIANS FIND SAFETY NOT IN THE ABSENCE OF DANGER BUT IN THE PRESENCE OF GOD.

Looking unto Jesus, the author and finisher of our faith.

HEBREWS 12:2

Every workman takes pride in a project completed and well-done. I thought of this recently when I visited the site of a new house my friend was building. The foundation had been laid, the walls erected, and the wiring and plumbing installed, but the structure still wasn't a house. It needed the finishers. Without the woodworkers, the cabinetmakers, the carpet layers, and the painters, the building was incomplete.

We as Christians need a "finisher" too. The sanctifying work of the Holy Spirit in our lives, which began at conversion, must continue until the One who began the transformation finishes it. And that can happen only by trusting and obeying Jesus, "the author and finisher of our faith," the One to whom we are being conformed.

God is not the architect of incompleteness. The Bible says, "He who has begun a good work in you will complete it until the day of Jesus Christ" (Phil. 1:6). Our part is to stay in fellowship with Him. He'll do the rest. —P. R. V.

**KEEP IN STEP WITH GOD; HE HAS
PLANNED EVERY STEP OF THE WAY.**

The LORD of hosts, Him you shall hallow; let Him be your fear.

ISAIAH 8:13

On June 6, 1944, five thousand ships departed England for the Normandy coast and the greatest invasion of World War II. From this military event comes the story of the skipper who lectured his crew on fear, and said, "Fear is a very healthy thing." A third-class yeoman yelled in reply, "Captain, you're looking at the healthiest sailor in the United States Navy."

We tend to associate fear with punishment and danger, but that shows our limited understanding of it. Perfect fear comes from our sense of awe and wonder as we get glimpses of God. John says, "Perfect love casts out fear" (1 John 4:18). Fear, for the Christian, is not so much about punishment as love. God-fearing people are God-loving people. —D. J. D.

THE FEAR OF GOD CAN DELIVER US FROM THE FEAR OF MEN.

*So this Daniel prospered in the reign
of Darius and in the reign of Cyrus.*

DANIEL 6:28

Oswald Chambers of Scotland showed so much artistic promise that he was invited to study under Europe's greatest masters at age eighteen. But he declined the offer and enrolled in a little-known Bible school, where he eventually became a teacher. Later, he went to Egypt and ministered to the spiritual needs of British soldiers. Chambers died there when he was only in his forties, but he left to the world a rich legacy of devotional literature.

Daniel began his career as a young captive in Babylon. Repeatedly he put his life on the line to remain faithful to the Lord. He refused to compromise, and God elevated him to a position of prominence. Both men made doing God's will their prime objective; both achieved success. —H. V. L.

**OUTSIDE GOD'S WILL IS NO TRUE
SUCCESS; IN GOD'S WILL, NO FAILURE.**

Those who wait on the LORD . . . shall run and not be weary.

ISAIAH 40:31

Astronaut Michael Collins described the problem of trying to link two orbiting space vehicles. When two airplanes rendezvous for an in-flight refueling, the plane behind simply increases speed until it catches the other aircraft. In outer space, however, the situation is quite different. Acceleration puts the trailing spacecraft into a higher orbit, causing it to move away and widen the gap. Therefore, the ship's commander must act against all natural instincts and slow down, dropping his craft into a lower orbit, which enables him to catch up, maneuver into position, and make contact at precisely the right moment.

So it is with the busy child of God. Taking on more activities can mean losing ground as a result of lost time with the Lord. To get ahead, we must slow down and wait on the Lord. As we do, we will have time to pray, to read God's Word, and to rearrange our priorities.
—M. R. D. II

**THOSE WHO WAIT FOR THE WILL OF
GOD, REST IN THE WORK OF GOD.**

The will of the Lord be done.

ACTS 21:14

In the early 1940s, the president of Dallas Seminary, Lewis Chafer, gave a very brief banquet speech. Introduced after a long program, he announced his subject: "The Reasonableness of Fully Surrendering Our Lives to God." Then, because of the lateness of the hour, he gave only the three points of his message.

Reason 1: God is all-wise and knows better than anyone else what is best for my life.

Reason 2: He is almighty and has the power to accomplish what is best for me.

Reason 3: God loves me more than anyone else does.

Chafer concluded, "Therefore the most logical thing I can do is surrender my life to God. What more can I say? What more need I say?"

No matter what happens, when we do God's will we're in the safest place in all the world. —H. V. L.

SURRENDER MEANS VICTORY WHEN WE SURRENDER TO GOD.

He who has seen Me has seen the Father.

JOHN 14:9

When he was only 13 years old, violinist Yehudi Menuhin was invited to perform with the Berlin Philharmonic Symphony Orchestra. With distinguished musicians in the audience listening to him, the youthful genius played some of the most difficult compositions by Beethoven, Bach, and Brahms.

The response was so enthusiastic that the management called in the police in case the crowd got out of control. Albert Einstein, who had listened with utter delight to the prodigy, avoided the authorities by running across the stage into Yehudi's dressing room. He embraced the surprised violinist and exclaimed, "Now I know there is a God in heaven!"

While the beauty of music does indeed bear witness to God's reality, only through the supernatural life and ministry of Christ recorded in the Gospels are we able to know God with unshadowed certainty. We read the Gospels and we exclaim with awe and adoration, "Now we know there is a God in heaven!" —V. C. G.

CHRIST BRIDGED THE GAP BETWEEN THE INFINITE GOD AND FINITE MAN.

Godliness with contentment is great gain.

1 TIMOTHY 6:6

Over the past 15 years, a New Jersey businessman has anonymously given away more than $600 million to universities, medical centers, and other beneficiaries. When a legal complication forced him to reveal his identity, he explained his generosity by saying, "Nobody can wear two pairs of shoes at one time. I simply decided I had enough money."

A friend of the donor described him as a man who doesn't own a house or a car, flies economy class, wears a $15 watch, and "didn't want his money to crush him."

Few people seem able to treat their resources as a servant instead of a master. It seems so natural and sensible to grasp rather than to give. Even as followers of Christ, we may mistakenly believe that "godliness is a means of gain" (1 Tim. 6:5). But the apostle Paul wrote, "Godliness with contentment is great gain. . . . And having food and clothing, with these we shall be content" (vv. 6, 8). —D. C. M

MONEY IS WHAT YOU MAKE IT—A MASTER OR A SERVANT.

He who gives a right answer kisses the lips.

PROVERBS 24:26

During one of his sermons, Hudson Taylor, pioneer missionary to China, filled a glass with water and placed it on a table in front of him. While he was speaking, he pounded his fist hard enough to make the water splash onto the table. He then explained, "You will come up against much trouble. But when you do, remember, only what's in you will spill out."

That's worth thinking about, isn't it? When we are mistreated or misunderstood, how do we respond? With loving words, patience, and kindness? Or are we inclined to retaliate in anger?

When we live under the control of the Holy Spirit, we will show it by the way we react to the jolting trials and temptations of life. If our heart is full of the Savior's love, we will respond to the jostling of an unexpected trial with patience and kindness. Like a full glass of water, what's inside of us will spill over on the outside. —R. W. D.

WHEN TROUBLE GROWS, YOUR CHARACTER SHOWS.

Though he fall, he shall not be utterly cast down.

PSALM 37:24

*P*aul Wylie was skating in the 1988 Winter Olympics at Calgary. He was nervous as he began his program before 20,000 people and a TV audience of millions. Then, in his first jump, something went wrong. He writes, "A flash later my hand touches the ice; the blade will not hold. I start slipping and now I realize it: I am falling. All I hear as I collapse to the ice is the empathetic groan of what seems like a million voices."

Wylie was faced with a split-second choice: He could focus on the mistake and give up, or he could keep on skating and do his best. Just then this Scripture verse came to his mind: "Though he fall, he shall not be utterly cast down" (Ps. 37:24). He continued his routine and decided to skate "heartily, as to the Lord" (Col. 3:23). At program's end the crowd burst into enthusiastic applause for his courage and determination.

It's one thing to fall; it's quite another to give up. —D. C. E.

SUCCESS CONSISTS OF GETTING UP JUST ONE MORE TIME THAN YOU'VE FALLEN DOWN.

*We . . . shall be caught up together with
them in the clouds to meet the Lord.*

1 THESSALONIANS 4:17

Nineteenth-century evangelist D. L. Moody loved to tell a story about the fishermen who ventured far out on the Adriatic Sea. Each evening their wives would go down to the shore to await their husbands' return after a long and perilous day.

Standing there, they would sing the first verse of a familiar hymn, then pause and listen intently. They knew their husbands were safe when they heard them singing the second verse as it was carried by the wind across the waves.

I like to think that even as we long to see our loved ones who have gone to heaven, they are eagerly awaiting the day when we'll be together again. One of these days, whether we are "caught up together with them in the clouds" or we pass through death's valley, we're going to have a great and grand reunion. —R. W. D.

DEATH CANNOT SEPARATE THOSE WHO ARE ONE IN CHRIST.

*I have given you an example, that you
should do as I have done to you.*

JOHN 13:15

In washing the disciples' feet, Jesus shocked His followers. This was not the beginning of the first valet school; Jesus was not some water-basin wonder. With a towel around His waist, Jesus washed soiled feet, but He was more interested in dirty people than dusty toes.

The disciples had been vying for leadership positions, and Jesus played chief foot-washer to clean their hearts rather than their feet. Jesus acted as a servant to combat the hotshot attitudes of the disciples. He hoped they would recall and imitate His humility.

In coming to this earth, Jesus became part of a long-running play, but He was not acting. He took the servant part for some thirty-three years to show people how to live (Phil. 2:7). Those who follow Him lead by example. They never make a grand entrance; they come in through the service door. —D. J. D.

**GETTING OUR OWN WAY SERVES ONLY
TO GET IN THE WAY OF SERVICE.**

I have prayed for you, that your faith should not fail.

LUKE 22:32

With cranberries, it's the bounce that counts. According to *Science Digest*, processing cranberries involves pouring freshly picked berries down a series of step-like boards. At each level, only those berries that bounce over an eight- to ten-inch barrier pass the test. Each berry gets eleven chances. Those that fail are discarded. Some fruits are judged by firmness and color, but the cranberry is distinguished by its ability to "bounce like a golf ball."

The strength of our faith can also be judged by our ability to bounce back after defeat. Although setbacks hurt, they allow us to show our underlying confidence in Christ. A spiritual reversal should not cause us to give up. It's the "bounce" of our faith and His forgiveness that are important. —M. R. D. II

DEFEAT ISN'T BITTER UNLESS WE SWALLOW IT.

There is a lad here who has five barley loaves and two small fish.

JOHN 6:9

About halfway through a rehearsal conducted by Sir Michael Costa, with trumpets blaring, drums rolling, and violins singing their rich melody, the piccolo player muttered to himself, "What good am I doing? I might just as well not be playing. Nobody can hear me anyway." So he kept the instrument to his mouth, but he made no sound. Within moments, the conductor cried, "Stop! Stop! Where's the piccolo?"

At certain times in life we all feel insignificant and useless. Surrounded by people with greater talent than ours, we are tempted in our weak moments just to settle back and "let George do it." We forget that Jesus used five loaves and two small fish to feed a multitude.

Whether our talent is great or small, the performance isn't complete until we do our best with what we have. —R. W. D.

IN GOD'S EYES IT IS A GREAT THING TO DO A LITTLE THING WELL.

Let us not grow weary while doing good.

GALATIANS 6:9

As Hitler was mounting his attack against England during World War II, Winston Churchill was asked to speak to a group of discouraged Londoners. He uttered an eight-word encouragement: "Never give up! Never, never, never give up!"

There will be times when you'll be discouraged in your Christian walk, but you must never, never, never give up. If nothing else, your struggle against sin will cause you to turn to God again and again and cling to Him in your desperation.

What's required is dogged endurance, keeping at the task of obedience through the ebbs and flows, ups and downs, victories and losses in life. It is trying again, while knowing that God is working in you to accomplish His purposes (Phil. 1:6; 2:13). It is persistently pursuing God's will for your life till you stand before Him and your work is done. —D. H. R.

PERSEVERANCE CAN TIP THE SCALES FROM FAILURE TO SUCCESS.

The LORD had blessed Abraham in all things.

GENESIS 24:1

The 2000 US presidential election was finally decided after weeks of recounts, court battles, and controversy about punch-card ballots. Political pundits and comedians had a heyday. Even after the Florida recount wrangling was over, a billboard along a Michigan highway reminded travelers of those post-election days. It carried this clever message: "Count your blessings. Recount if necessary."

In Genesis 24:1 we read that "the LORD had blessed Abraham in all things." Remarkable! The brief biography of Abraham's 175 years (11:29–25:8) reveals blessing after blessing interwoven through all the adversities, testings, and even failures of his life.

As we review our years, whether many or few, we can see that same wonderful mixture of blessings, promises, and mercy running through our lives, even the trials and lapses of faith. If we can't, maybe a recount is necessary. —D. J. D.

PRAISE TO GOD COMES NATURALLY WHEN YOU COUNT YOUR BLESSINGS.

"Peace, be still!"

MARK 4:39

*B*reton fishermen on the coast of France have a brief prayer that humbly acknowledges God's control of nature and life: "God, your sea is so great and my boat is so small." In recognizing that the sea belongs to God, the fishermen see God as the only source of safety for their boats.

In calming the Sea of Galilee, Jesus taught the disciples not only about His power over nature but also about external and internal peace. The lesson about external peace was the easier of the two; He stopped the storm. Dealing with the storm inside the disciples was more difficult; fear had replaced the disciples' faith.

Trust and tranquility are twins in the spiritual life. Perfect peace comes from complete trust (Isa. 26:3). —D. J. D.

BETTER THE STORM WITH CHRIST THAN SMOOTH WATERS WITHOUT HIM.

NOVEMBER 30

When [Jesus] saw the multitudes, He was moved with compassion for them.

MATTHEW 9:36

While on furlough from missionary service in Africa, Robert Moffat (1795–1883) spoke in England about his work. A young medical student in the audience had hoped to serve on the mission field in China, but that land was closed. He listened as Moffat described a frequent sight in Africa. "There is a vast plain to the north, where I have sometimes seen, in the morning sun, the smoke of a thousand villages where no missionary has ever been."

"The smoke of a thousand villages." Those words painted a vivid picture and gripped the heart of the young student. This was the challenge he was looking for in his desire to reach the unreached. Filled with a new vision, the young man went to Moffat and asked, "Would I do for Africa?" That student was David Livingstone. Workers are still needed today. —R. W. D.

WE CAN REACH OUT TO A WORLD IN NEED WITH THE WORD IT NEEDS!

December

God reigns over the nations; God sits on His holy throne.

PSALM 47:8

During the days of the Cold War, this startling headline appeared in *The Grand Rapids Press:* Computer Error Could Start War.

The article that followed was equally alarming. It reported: "For the second time in 7 months, a computer at the nation's missile warning center erroneously put US strategic forces on alert against a Soviet missile attack on the United States."

The idea of nuclear war is horrifying enough, but to think that it could be caused by a computer mistake is even more appalling. We who believe in the God of the Bible, however, know that He has not abdicated His throne, and that everything is under His control. He's aware of what's going on, and nothing can happen to violate His sovereignty. The long-range good that God has in mind for all who love Him cannot be thwarted.

The Lord God reigns! —R. W. D.

EVERYTHING IS IN GOD'S HANDS. LEAVE IT THERE.

*Bethlehem Ephrathah, . . . out of you shall come
forth to Me the One to be Ruler in Israel.*

MICAH 5:2

Isaiah, Micah, and many of the other prophets foretold many details of Jesus' birth, life, and death hundreds of years before they were fulfilled. The likelihood of these events occurring exactly as they were prophesied is too remote to explain away the phenomenon by calling it coincidence.

In *Science Speaks*, Peter Stoner applies the modern science of probability to just eight prophecies. He said, "The chance that any man might have . . . fulfilled all eight prophecies is one in ten to the seventh degree. That would be 1 in 100,000,000,000,000,000." Stoner said that if we took that many silver dollars and laid them across Texas they would cover the state two feet deep.

Since Christ's first coming was the exact fulfillment of many prophecies, we can expect the same of His second coming. —D. J. D.

PROPHECY IS HISTORY WRITTEN AHEAD OF TIME.

*There is joy in the presence of the angels
of God over one sinner who repents.*

LUKE 15:10

istory was unfolding before our eyes. There on our TV
screens were pictures of East Germans dancing on top of
the Berlin Wall. We didn't know these people personally. We were
separated by miles, culture, and language. Yet we rejoiced with them
as they felt the invigorating breeze of freedom blow across their land.

A people had been given a new measure of liberty, and we
shared their thrilling moment. The wall was coming down, an era of
tyranny was ending, and free people everywhere celebrated with those
jubilant East Germans.

This reminded me of another vicarious celebration—the joy
that the angels in heaven experience when a sinner breathes his first
breath of freedom from the tyranny of sin. Because the insurmountable
wall that separates man from God has been torn down by Christ on
the cross, we can now be free from the oppressive weight of sin's guilt.
This burden, which makes it impossible to enjoy life, is lifted when a
person receives Christ as his or her Savior. And how the angels rejoice!
—J. D. B.

ANGELS REJOICE WHEN SINNERS REPENT.

Thanks be to God for His indescribable gift!

2 CORINTHIANS 9:15

In the early 19th century, a war-weary world was anxiously watching the march of Napoleon. But during that time, obscure, seemingly insignificant events were occurring that would help to shape the future.

In 1809, between the battles of Trafalgar and Waterloo, William E. Gladstone was born in Liverpool; Alfred, Lord Tennyson in Summersby, England; Oliver Wendell Holmes in Boston; Felix Mendelssohn in Hamburg, Germany; and Abraham Lincoln in Hodgenville, Kentucky. Now, 200 years later, is there the slightest doubt about the greater contribution to history—those battles or those babies?

So it was with the birth of Jesus. The Bethlehem crowd was all concerned about a census and the power of Rome. They had no inkling that the infinite infant Son of God was asleep in their little town. Only a few shepherds hurried to see Him who was born in a stable. And as they left, they glorified God. —D. J. D.

GOD'S GIFT TO A DYING WORLD IS THE LIFE-GIVING SAVIOR.

We are hard-pressed on every side, yet not crushed.

2 CORINTHIANS 4:8

Explorer Samuel Hearne and his party had just set out on a rigorous expedition in northern Canada to find the mouth of the Coppermine River. A few days after they left, thieves stole most of their supplies. Hearne's response to the apparent misfortune can inspire us all, for he wrote, "The weight of our baggage being lightened, our next day's journey was more swift and pleasant."

Paul too knew what it was to face all sorts of perilous circumstances (2 Cor. 11:26). And time and time again he turned to Lord for His deliverance and provision.

How about you? How did you respond the last time you learned that the refrigerator needed to be replaced or the car engine had to be rebuilt? When things go wrong, ask God for strength and wisdom. Then thank Him for working to perfect your faith. —D. C. E.

UNDER THE CIRCUMSTANCES? LEARN TO LIVE ABOVE THEM!

Unto us a Child is born, unto us a Son is given. . . .
And His name will be called Wonderful.

ISAIAH 9:6

Throughout the centuries since Jesus' birth, man has marveled at the wonder of His person and work. An unknown author declared:

"He became a man that we might become the sons of God. In infancy He troubled a king. In boyhood He puzzled the teachers. In manhood He ruled the course of nature, He walked upon the billows, hushed the sea to sleep, and healed the multitudes without medicine.

"He never wrote a book, yet the libraries of the world are filled with volumes that have been written about Him. He never penned a musical note, yet He is the theme of more songs than any other subject.

"Great men have come and gone, yet He lives on. Herod could not kill Him. Satan could not seduce Him. All others have failed in some way, but not Jesus! This perfect One is altogether lovely." He is matchless in His person and work. He is our Savior. —H. G. B.

PONDER THE WONDER OF JESUS.

*It is good that one should hope and wait
quietly for the salvation of the LORD.*

LAMENTATIONS 3:26

*O*ur fast-moving world demands immediate service—instant car-phone communication with fax capabilities, 20-minute pizza delivery service, one-hour film development. Waiting is grating.

As a result, we don't have time for breakdowns, recuperation, or repairs. If something goes wrong, we want a quick fix so we can be on our way. If stores can't give us instant service, we take our business elsewhere. Whether it's new brakes or a calm for jangled nerves, we want fast action or instant relief.

This demand for quick fixes also spills over into the spiritual realm. When a relationship breaks down, we want to quick-fix it with a mumbled apology or a cheap gift. Or when trouble comes and our lives begin to unravel, we expect to solve the problem with a hasty prayer.

The psalmist David wanted release from his distresses (Ps. 25:17), but he prayed, "On You I wait all the day" (v. 5). He ended his plea for help by saying, "I wait for You" (v. 21). —D. C. E.

GOD'S CLOCK IS NEVER SLOW, BUT OURS IS OFTEN FAST.

You, O God, have tested us; You have
refined us as silver is refined.

PSALM 66:10

talented violinist was scheduled to play before a very critical audience. Although she had a fine instrument, she was not satisfied with the quality of its sound. So she said to her father, "This violin must yield its full resonance and vibration of tone. I'm going out to buy some tested strings."

When asked what tested strings were, she replied, "First they're put on a rack and stretched and strained to take all the vacillation out of them. Then they are hammered and put through an acid test. This is what enables them to produce a perfect and full tone." When she attached the tested strings and tuned the instrument, the music was noticeably more warm and rich than before.

If our lives are going to produce beautiful music for the Lord, testing is imperative. Although we don't enjoy the stretch, the strain, and the stress, what God-honoring results they can produce! —P. R. V.

**THE TRIALS OF LIFE ARE INTENDED
TO MAKE US BETTER, NOT BITTER.**

Glory, honor, and peace to everyone who works what is good.

ROMANS 2:10

According to the book *Life of Francis d'Assisi,* Francis once invited a young monk to join him on a trip to town to preach. Honored to be given the invitation, the monk readily accepted.

All day long he and Francis walked through the streets, byways, and alleys, and even into the suburbs. They rubbed shoulders with hundreds of people. At day's end, the two headed back home. Not even once had Francis addressed a crowd, nor had he talked to anyone about the gospel. Greatly disappointed, his young companion said, "I thought we were going into town to preach." Francis responded, "My son, we have preached. We were preaching while we were walking. We were seen by many and our behavior was closely watched. It is of no use to walk anywhere to preach unless we preach everywhere as we walk!"

Most people cannot preach, in the usual sense of the term. But we all do "talk" through our daily walk. So, let's watch our step!

—R. W. D.

ACTIONS SPEAK LOUDER THAN WORDS.

Then the shepherds returned, . . . praising God
for all the things that they had heard and seen.

LUKE 2:20

*I*n a delightful sermon titled, "When the Angels Were
Gone," G. L. Chappell emphasizes that when the angels
announced the good news to the shepherds the men took action.
They went to Bethlehem to see the Christ-child for themselves.

Chappell then sets up a hypothetical situation in which the
shepherds respond quite differently. They simply sit around discussing
the brightness of the angelic appearance and the wonder of the message.

Some 40 years later, one of the shepherds tells his small grandson
about that eventful night. The youngster asks, "But Granddaddy, was
what the angels said really true?" The shepherd continues telling him
what he has heard about Jesus, even the reports of His resurrection.
But when the lad keeps asking, all the elderly shepherd can do is
shake his head and say, "I don't really know. I never went to see."

Many people are like that shepherd. They have heard about
Jesus but they have never come to Him. —H. V. L.

WHEN YOU LOOK TO THE LIGHT YOU RECEIVE ETERNAL LIFE.

Happy is he who has the God of Jacob for his help.

PSALM 146:5

The foundation for happiness is a proper relationship with the Lord. But to fully experience that happiness, we must build on that foundation in practical ways. I found this list of "Ten Rules for Happier Living" in an issue of *Pulpit Helps*.

1. Give something away (no strings attached).
2. Do a kindness (and forget it).
3. Spend time with the aged (experience is priceless).
4. Look intently into the face of a baby (and marvel).
5. Laugh often (it is life's lubricant).
6. Give thanks (a thousand times a day is not enough).
7. Pray (or you will lose the way).
8. Work (with vim and vigor).
9. Plan as though you will live forever (you will).
10. Live as though you will die tomorrow (because you will die on some tomorrow).

Those are excellent ideas for happier living. Try them. They work!

—R. W. D.

TRUSTING AND OBEYING THE LORD BRINGS TRUE HAPPINESS.

He has put a new song in my mouth.

PSALM 40:3

The song of the humpback whale is one of the strangest in nature. It is a weird combination of high- and low-pitched groanings. Those who have studied the humpback whale say their songs are noteworthy because these giants of the deep are continually changing them. New patterns are added and old ones eliminated so that over a period of time the whale actually sings a whole new song.

There's a sense in which the Christian should be continually composing new songs of praise around the fresh mercies of God. Unfortunately, many of us just keep singing the "same old song." Most certainly, we must repeatedly affirm the fundamentals of our faith. But as the psalmist tells us, the works of God's deliverance in the lives of His people are many, and give us reason to express our praise to Him in new ways. His works are more than we can count (Ps. 40:5).

—M. R. D. II

SEEING GOD'S WORK IN OUR LIVES PUTS A NEW SONG ON OUR LIPS.

They have devoted themselves to the ministry of the saints.

1 CORINTHIANS 16:15

An America's Cup yacht has a crew of 16 people, including the navigator, the helmsman, and the mastmen. But the boat could not compete without the relentless work of the five "grinders"—the men who turn the heavy cranks that control the sails.

In a *USA Today* article, a grinder described his role this way: "A grinder at the America's Cup level is similar to a tight end in football. We need strength to provide the physical energy to power the boat around the race course. Essentially, our job is to turn the handles to raise and lower the sails and jibe/tack the sails from one side of the boat to the other."

In the work of Christ, many jobs get noticed. Some have to do with determining strategy, others with steering the course. But unless there are a lot of grinders—those men and women who are willing to work faithfully at the unglamorous roles—His work cannot go forward. So if you are a grinder, keep at it! Your faithfulness is far more important than you realize. Our Captain is depending on you!
—D. C. E.

THE WORLD CROWNS SUCCESS; GOD CROWNS FAITHFULNESS.

Your adversary the devil walks about . . .
seeking whom he may devour.

1 PETER 5:8

In the Australian bush country grows a little plant called the "sundew." It has a slender stem and tiny, round leaves fringed with hairs that glisten with bright drops of liquid as delicate as fine dew. Woe to the insect, however, that dares to dance on it. Although its attractive clusters of red, white, and pink blossoms are harmless, the leaves are deadly. The shiny moisture on each leaf is sticky and will imprison any bug that touches it. As an insect struggles to free itself, the vibration causes the leaves to close tightly around it. This innocent-looking plant then feeds on its victim.

As we journey down life's path, we must beware of Satan's enticements to sin. They will appear inviting and harmless, but they are deadly traps. We must be on our guard at all times and depend on the Lord for His help and strength. —H. G. B.

COMBAT SATAN'S DECEPTION WITH SPIRITUAL DISCERNMENT.

The Word became flesh and dwelt among us.

JOHN 1:14

Robert Stevenson, grandfather of the famous Scottish author Robert Louis Stevenson, was respected in his own right as a gifted engineer. In 1872, 100 years after he was born, a celebration was arranged to honor his memory.

As part of the festivities, a parade was held displaying many banners. One of them stood out as best expressing the spirit of that occasion. It was held high by a farmer, and it bore this simple message: ONE OF US. The common people found great joy in the fact that Stevenson was identified with them.

That story brings to mind Philippians 2. When the eternal Son of God was born in a lowly stable in Bethlehem, He came as one of us. He came "in the likeness of men" (v. 7) so that He might live and die in our place. —R. W. D.

NO GOD, NO PEACE; KNOW GOD, KNOW PEACE.

Be tenderhearted, be courteous.

1 PETER 3:8

I remember reading a story about a plainly dressed man who entered a church in the Netherlands and took a seat near the front. A few minutes later a woman walked down the aisle, saw the stranger in the place she always sat, and curtly asked him to leave. He quietly got up and moved to a section reserved for the poor.

When the meeting was over, a friend of the woman asked her if she knew the man she had ordered out of her seat. "No," she replied. Her friend then informed her, "The man you ordered out of your seat was King Oscar of Sweden! He is here visiting the Queen."

The woman was greatly embarrassed and wished she had shown the king the courtesy of giving up her seat. But it was too late. He had left.

Courtesy blossoms in a heart that is humble. —H. G. B.

GENTLENESS AND COURTESY DESCRIBE HOW WE SHOULD BE.

[Abraham] was called the friend of God.

JAMES 2:23

As a young man, Joseph Scriven had been engaged to a woman he deeply loved. But tragedy struck the night before their wedding when the boat she was in capsized and she drowned. In the hope of forgetting the shock, which he never did, Joseph left his home in Ireland and went to Canada.

There he taught school and served as a tutor. He chose to live very simply, spending his money and strength in generously providing for destitute people. He was considered an eccentric by some, yet all he tried to do was obey God's Word as best he could understand it.

In his loneliness, Joseph Scriven needed a steadfast friend. Having found that friend in Jesus Christ, he wrote these simple words, which movingly express his experience:

> What a friend we have in Jesus,
> All our sins and griefs to bear!
> What a privilege to carry
> Everything to God in prayer!
> —V. C. G.

FAITH IN CHRIST IS FAITH IN AN UNFAILING FRIEND.

All Scripture is given by inspiration of God.

2 TIMOTHY 3:16

The story is told about a young boy named Timothy who was planning to give his grandmother a Bible for Christmas. He wanted to write something special on the flyleaf but wasn't sure what to say. So he decided to copy what he had seen in a book his father had received from a friend.

Christmas morning came and Grandmother opened her gift. She was not only pleased to receive the Bible, but she was amused by the inscription Timothy had put in it. It read: "To Grandma, with compliments of the author."

Knowing who wrote a book often determines whether we'll pick it up and read it. The Bible, with its divine origin, not only ought to be read, but it demands our respect, our trust, and our obedience. It comes "with compliments of the Author." —R. W. D.

THE BIBLE IS A GIFT FROM THE AUTHOR—GOD.

The merciful man does good for his own soul.

PROVERBS 11:17

Author James Duff tells of the time when English pastor and theologian Andrew Fuller (1754–1815) was collecting money for foreign missions. One of his contacts was an old friend. When presented with the need, the man said, "Well, Andrew, seeing it's you, I'll give you 5 pounds."

"No," said Fuller, "I can't take your money for my cause, seeing it is for me," and he handed the money back.

The man saw his point. "Andrew, you are right. Here's 10 pounds, seeing it is for Jesus Christ."

Duff concluded, "Let us remember, it is not the amount we give toward helping the Lord's work; it is the motive He looks at."

The Lord is more concerned with why we give than with how much we give. —R. W. D.

GOD SEES THE GIVER AS WELL AS THE GIFT—
THE HEART AS WELL AS THE HAND.

The city had no need of the sun or of the moon to
shine in it, for the glory of God illuminated it.

REVELATION 21:23

The University of Colorado's Fiske Planetarium needed money, so its director dreamed up a comical fund-raiser. He printed brochures that offered 1,000-acre lots on the planet Mars for only $20.

The flier read: "This land steal features pink skies, unlimited rock gardens, and not one but two moons. So peaceful, quiet, and romantic—even the natives are friendly." The literature promised, "At one-sixth the gravity of Earth, your golf game will improve immensely—drives will be six times longer. Mars will provide a world of adventure for the entire family." The gag was surprisingly successful. People across the country sent in $20 for a deed, for space flight insurance, and for a simulated sample of red Martian soil.

If this story catches your imagination, then think about the ultimate real estate—heaven! —M. R. D. II

GOD OPENS THE DOOR OF HEAVEN TO ALL
WHO OPEN THEIR HEARTS TO HIM.

The virgin shall be with child, and bear a Son,
and they shall call His name Immanuel.

MATTHEW 1:22

Many Christians complain that Christmas is "too commercial." Yes, Christmas has become very commercial. But as we purchase and wrap gifts, every present can be a silent testimony to the supreme gift, God's "only begotten Son" (John 3:16).

Yes, we know that Santa is a myth and that reindeer don't fly. It's pure fiction. But instead of griping about these nonessentials, which only focuses on them, we need to call attention to the truth of the Baby who was born in Bethlehem.

And what about the cry to put Christ back into Christmas? Well, He never left. Listen to the words of the carols heard over and over in stores, malls, and on the streets. They proclaim more truth in one holiday than many pulpits do in 3 months. They put into the minds of young and old the wonderful truth that "the Lord is come" and that He is to be adored. —D. C. E.

To see the real meaning of Christmas, focus on Christ.

Pray for those who spitefully use you and persecute you.

MATTHEW 5:44

During the war in Kosovo in 1999, three Americans were captured and held hostage for more than a month. After intense negotiations, a breakthrough occurred and the prisoners were allowed to go free.

Roy Lloyd was part of the delegation that secured their release. He reported, "Each of the three young soldiers was very religious. One of them, Christopher Stone, would not leave until he was allowed to go back to the soldier who served as his guard and pray for him."

Here was a young man who knew something about the principles of Jesus. He could have resented his circumstances and hated his captors. He could have developed a bitter, vengeful spirit. He could have carried a burning rage out of that difficulty. But following the command of Jesus (Matt. 5:44) and the example of Paul and Silas in Philippi (Acts 16:25–34), he forgave his captor and ministered to him. —D. C. E.

**WE ARE NEVER MORE CHRISTLIKE THAN
WHEN WE CHOOSE TO FORGIVE.**

Unto us a Child is born, unto us a Son is given.

ISAIAH 9:6

In December 1903, after many attempts, the Wright brothers were successful in getting their "flying machine" off the ground. Thrilled, they telegraphed this message to their sister Katherine: "We have actually flown 120 feet. Will be home for Christmas."

Katherine hurried to the editor of the local newspaper and showed him the message. He glanced at it and said, "How nice. The boys will be home for Christmas." He totally missed the big news—man had flown!

Many people today make a similar mistake when they hear the word *Christmas.* They don't think of Jesus and His miraculous birth. Instead, they think of family gatherings, festive meals, decorations, and gifts. To them, Christmas brings nostalgia and memories of childhood.

Family celebrations are wonderful, but if that's all Christmas means to us, we are missing its true significance. —R. W. D.

TAKE CARE IN KEEPING CHRISTMAS, NOT TO LOSE CHRIST.

He came and preached peace.

EPHESIANS 2:17

It was the night before Christmas in 1870. French and German armies faced each other on the field of battle in the Franco-Prussian War. A French soldier started walking toward the German lines. His comrades watched breathlessly, expecting to hear at any instant the crack of a rifle that would end his life. As he neared the enemy lines, he stopped and began singing, "Noel, noel! Noel, noel! Born is the King of Israel!" No shot rang out.

Slowly the Frenchman returned to his ranks. There was silence! Then from the German side came a lone soldier to that same spot and sang the German version of the same song. After each stanza both armies united in the chorus. For a few minutes Christ brought peace to that battlefield.

God is a peacemaker who always takes the first step. Jesus came as a baby, and when He grew to manhood He preached peace to a warring world. Then, in the greatest peace initiative this world has ever seen, Christ made peace between God and man by dying for our sins (Col. 1:20).
—D. J. D.

THE WORLD NEEDS THE PEACE THAT PASSES ALL MISUNDERSTANDING.

*You shall call His name Jesus, for He
will save His people from their sins.*

MATTHEW 1:21

Two thousand years ago, there were no earthly plans for celebrating Jesus' birth. Quietly and unannounced, Joseph and Mary entered Bethlehem and searched for a place to spend the night.

It was a busy time in the Judean village, but the excitement had nothing to do with the upcoming birth. The crowds had gathered to take part in a census. They didn't know that Mary was about to deliver the Savior.

As the year 2000 approached, the story had changed. There were serious discussions going on about how Bethlehem could get ready for the estimated 4 million tourists who would converge on the Israeli city during Christmas 2000. What a contrast to that first Christmas!

We can make all the plans we want to, but the best way to celebrate Jesus' birthday is by trusting Him as Savior. —J. D. B.

CHRIST WAS BORN THAT WE MIGHT BE BORN AGAIN.

*Walk in wisdom toward those who
are outside, redeeming the time.*

COLOSSIANS 4:5

If we live 65 years, we have about 600,000 hours at our disposal. Assuming we are 18 when we complete high school, we have 47 years, or nearly 412,000 hours to live after graduation.

If we spend 8 hours a day sleeping, 8 hours for personal, social, and recreational activities, and 8 hours for working, that amounts to 137,333 hours in each category. When we think of the time we have to work and play in terms of hours, it doesn't seem like much. And when seen in the light of eternity, it's but a fleeting moment. How important, therefore, that we spend our waking hours wisely!

D. J. De Pree, a former member of the RBC Board of Directors always calculated his age in terms of days. If you asked him, "How old are you?" he answered immediately with the number of days. He based this practice on Psalm 90:12, "Teach us to number our days, that we may gain a heart of wisdom." Literally counting his days reminded him of the swift passage of time and the need to live with eternity's values in view. —R. W. D.

FUTURE PROSPECTS BRING PRESENT JOYS.

Do not forget to entertain strangers, for by so doing some have unwittingly entertained angels.

HEBREWS 13:2

In her book *Hidden Art,* Edith Schaeffer of L'Abri Fellowship tells of feeding the occasional vagrant who would stop at her back door and ask, "May I have a cup of coffee, ma'am, and maybe some bread?"

Edith would invite him to sit down, then go in to prepare a tray of food fit for a king: steaming soup and thick sandwiches, cut and arranged artfully on a plate with garnishes. The children would make a tiny bouquet, and if it was dusk, add a candle.

In amazement the man would gasp, "For me?" "Yes," Edith would answer, "and coffee will be ready in a minute. This Gospel of John is for you too. Take it with you. It really is very important."

How about serving up God's love to someone? —J. E. Y.

FOOD IS GOD'S LOVE MADE EDIBLE.

The disciples were first called Christians in Antioch.

ACTS 11:26

During an interview, the great Polish pianist Ignace Paderewski said, "It is not from choice that my life is music and nothing more, but when one is an artist what else can he be? When a whole lifetime is too short to attain the heights he wants to reach, how then can he devote any of the little time he has to things outside of his art?"

The interviewer then inquired, "And you have not yet attained the heights you seek?" "I am nothing!" replied the artist shaking his head. "If you could know the dream of what I would like to be, you would realize how little I have accomplished."

Paderewski's words spoke to me of the goal and attitude that every Christian should have. He had declared, "When one is an artist, what else can he be?" I would ask, "When one is a Christian, what else can he be?" —R. W. D.

**EVERY CHILD OF GOD SHOULD GROW
IN LIKENESS TO THE SON OF GOD.**

We will remember the name of the LORD our God.

PSALM 20:7

I was relieved to find out that I'm not the only one who forgets things. Everyone does at one time or another, according to Karen Bolla, a Johns Hopkins researcher. These are the things people most often forget:

➤	names	83%
➤	where something is	60%
➤	telephone numbers	57%
➤	words	53%
➤	what was said	49%
➤	faces	42%

And if you can't remember whether you've just done something, join 38 percent of the population.

Followers of Jesus Christ sometimes have a problem with forgetfulness. In high-pressure situations, or when we're just going through a daily routine, we seem to forget that we are God's children. We fail to recall what He has promised to do for us. We don't remember His awesome power and His love. David offered the solution in Psalm 20:7, "We will remember the name of the LORD our God." —D. C. E.

DAILY BLESSINGS ARE DAILY REMINDERS OF GOD.

*Teach us to number our days, that
we may gain a heart of wisdom.*

PSALM 90:12

The root meaning of the word translated *number* in
"teach us to number our days" (Ps. 90:12) is "to weigh"
or "to measure." We are to place each day in the balance and make
it tip the scales in a way that will bring glory to God and blessing
to the lives of others.

When the great artist Raphael died at the early age of 37,
friends and relatives carried his marvelous but unfinished painting,
The Transfiguration, in the funeral procession. His family felt that
because of the limited time he was allotted to use his creative genius,
the painting was an appropriate symbol of his unfulfilled earthly
aspirations.

That half-completed picture has another meaning—a message
that should impress itself on all of us: Life is fleeting. We should
treasure each hour as a gift of great value and use it to the best
advantage. —H. G. B.

INSTEAD OF COUNTING THE DAYS, MAKE YOUR DAYS COUNT.

You shine as lights in the world.

PHILIPPIANS 2:15

*W*hen Benjamin Franklin decided to interest the people of Philadelphia in street lighting, he hung a beautiful lantern on the end of a long bracket attached to the front of his house," wrote Cole D. Robinson in *World Horizons*. "He kept the glass brightly polished and carefully lit the wick each evening at the approach of dusk. Anyone walking on the dark street could see this light from a long way off and came under its warm glow."

What was the result? "It wasn't long before Franklin's neighbors began placing lamps outside their homes," Cole continued. "Soon the entire city realized the value of street lighting and followed his example with enthusiasm."

If we live according to the clear light of God's Word, God will dispel the darkness and others will be attracted to the Light. —H. G. B.

**LET'S NOT ONLY FOLLOW GOOD EXAMPLES,
LET'S BE GOOD EXAMPLES.**

OUR DAILY BREAD

Enjoy it everyday!

You can continue to make *Our Daily Bread* part of your regular time with God. Every month, you can receive a new booklet of devotional articles. Each day's topic is timely and the Bible teaching is reliable—just like the articles you've enjoyed in this book.

To receive *Our Daily Bread* each month at home, with no cost or obligation, just write to us at the address below, or visit us at **www.odb.org/guide** to order online.

As part of the *Our Daily Bread* family, you'll also get opportunities to receive Bible-study guides and booklets on a variety of topics, including creation, the church, and how to live the Christian life.

To order your copy of Our Daily Bread, write to us at:

RBC Ministries

RADIO BIBLE CLASS ~ FOUNDED 1938

USA: PO Box 2222, Grand Rapids, MI 49501-2222
CANADA: Box 1622, Windsor, ON N9A 6Z7

Notes

Prayers

Prayers

Notes

Prayers

Notes

Prayers